UK OCCUPATION AND EMPLOYMENT TRENDS TO 1990

An employer-based study of the trends and their underlying causes

Edited by
Amin Rajan and Richard Pearson

Butterworths
London Boston Durban Singapore Sydney Toronto Wellington

First published 1986

ⓒ Institute of Manpower Studies 1986

British Library Cataloguing in Publication Data

Institute of Manpower Studies
  UK occupation and employment trends to 1990
  an employer-based study of the trends
  and their underlying causes.
  1. Labor supply - Great Britain
  I. Title II. Occupations Study Group
  III. Rajan, Amin IV. Pearson, Richard, 1948-
  331.12'5'0941 HD5765.A6

  ISBN 0-408-02980-3

Library of Congress Cataloguing-in-Publication Data

UK occupation and employment trends to 1990.

  Bibliography: p.
  1. Employment forecasting--Great Britain.
  2. Great Britain--Occupations--Forecasting. 3. Manpower
  planning--Great Britain. I. Rajan, Amin, 1942-
  II. Pearson, Richard. III. Institute of Manpower
  Studies (Great Britain) IV. Occupations Study Group
  (Great Britain)
  HD5765.A6U38 1986 331.12'0941   86-13617
  ISBN 0-408-02980-3

Typeset by the Institute of Manpower Studies
Printed and Bound in Great Britain by
Mackays of Chatham Ltd.

Contents

FOREWORD

Change is everywhere in our national life, and many of the causes are readily recognisable as well as being extensively documented. One of the most obvious causes is technological advance; though a less visible feature of it is its quickening pace world-wide. To those close to science and technology this is not surprising. Discovery breeds invention and its applications exponentially, and the only limiting factors are available knowledge and human intellect. Social advances and easily observable social strains of the early eighties raised two issues in my mind. First, was the post-war regular cyclical pattern of job losses followed by compensatory gains any longer valid? Secondly, were the skills and occupational needs of the economy changing significantly? The implications of major shift could be profound.

All of us with an industrial or commercial interest in such issues have had to depend on economic forecasters for an independent view. As is well known, their answers are heavily influenced by the extrapolation of past trends. New developments tend to take time to feature in their models and I wondered whether there might be an alternative nationwide approach that could put due weight on recent developments in a way that would supplement the traditional methods.

It seemed to me that this could be achieved for a five-year forecast period by a confidential nationwide enquiry among employers of every kind on how they perceived their occupational needs. If you want to know about gainful occupations and employment, why not ask those who create both? After all, what employers do is ultimately the thing that will determine the outcome on the two issues.

Friends and colleagues urged me to canvass the notions in the first place among industrial and commercial leaders. The response was immediate and immensely supportive. These ideas must be tested they said. Most gratifying was their willingness to give financial backing to do so. Thus the Occupations Study Group (OSG) was born.

Frederick Meredith was seconded by IBM to become its Director and assist me. The Institute of Manpower Studies was engaged to carry out detailed enquiries on the basis of an agreed methodology. Arrangements were made in turn with the Centre for Urban and Regional Studies at Newcastle University to undertake a special exercise on small businesses.

Every step of the way along the road towards fulfillment of its aims, the Group has spared no effort to achieve credible objective results. The methodology of the study was carefully worked out through a feasibility study before the substantive field work was commissioned. The magnitude of the work may be judged by the fact that employers responding to enquiry covered in aggregate about half of the UK's working population.

We offer no recommendations for action. Recommending solutions to general and particular problems in the field of occupations and employment requires specialised knowledge and expertise as well as viewpoints beyond OSG's ambit. Our sole objective has been to pursue essential facts and data in the hope that they will be helpful to industry, commerce and academia as well as to those whose responsibility it is to take the actions that will provide the environment within which all can benefit.

If our results assist to these ends then the Group's efforts will have been amply justified, and further studies to update and expand the new database may be worth serious consideration.

Sir Austin Bide
Chairman, OSG

OSG SUPPORTING COMPANIES*

Abbey National Building Society
Allied-Lyons PLC
Baker Perkins PLC
Bass plc
BICC plc
Cable & Wireless plc
Cadbury Schweppes plc
Coopers & Lybrand
George Wimpey Plc
Guest Keen and Nettlefolds plc
Glaxo Holdings plc
Grand Metropolitan plc
Hill Samuel Group PLC
IBM United Kingdom Limited
International Computers Limited
Investors in Industry Group plc
John Laing plc
John Lewis Partnership Plc
Lex Service PLC
Lucas Industries plc
MEPC plc
Metal Box plc
Peugeot Talbot Motor Company Limited
Prudential Corporation plc
Racal Group Services Limited
Ranks Hovis McDougall plc
Scottish & Newcastle Breweries plc
Shell UK Limited
Smiths Industries plc
STC PLC
The BOC Group plc
The Rank Organisation plc
The Wellcome Foundation Ltd
Unigate PLC
Unilever PLC
Westland plc
Whitbread and Company PLC

STEERING COMMITTEE MEMBERS

Sir Austin Bide (Chairman), Sir Campbell Adamson, Professor Sir James Ball, C J Benson, Sir Basil Blackwell, Viscount Caldecote DSC, The Rt Hon Lord Carr of Hadley PC, Sir Henry Chilver, Sir Derrick Holden-Brown, Sir Trevor Holdsworth, F R Hurn, F W L Meredith, J M Raisman CBE, Geoffrey Tucker CBE.

* The policy of some supporting companies is to remain anonymous

OSG ACKNOWLEDGEMENTS

The names of those organisations and individuals who in various capacities and ways contributed to the work of OSG appear previously. To each and every one of them my profound gratitude for their support and advice.

In particular I wish to acknowledge my debt to the small band who bore the brunt. Frederick Meredith (and Sir Edwin Nixon of IBM who so kindly seconded him to OSG); Christopher Benson of MEPC who took charge of our finance and organised our charitability; Geoffrey Tucker whose constant advice was invaluable; Richard Pearson and Amin Rajan of IMS, without whose services nothing would have been achieved; their colleagues at Newcastle University; Jane Carver who ran the office for Frederick impeccably; my own secretaries, Brenda Davis and Stella Pache - whose help was tremendously valuable; and last but by no means least, Ian Armstrong, Ron Dodsworth, Peter Duffett and John Hillberry, whose help and advice were always available.

A special word of thanks to Stephen O'Brien, Chief Executive, Business in the Community who was a source of invaluable help, in particular at a moment of great need, when a rapid and concentrated follow-up of the postal enquiries became vitally urgent.

Sir Austin Bide

Chairman OSG

IMS ACKNOWLEDGEMENTS

This report is first and foremost the result of a team effort. Thanks are due to the Occupations Study Group for the funding of the project and Sir Austin Bide, Frederick Meredith (seconded from IBM), Ian Armstrong (seconded from BP), Jane Carver, and the Steering Group for their support and help throughout the project; and Peter Duffet (seconded from Prudential Assurance) for his unstinting efforts in co-ordinating local staff of Business in the Community support of the postal survey, without whose help we would not have achieved such a high survey response rate. The survey itself was processed by Monica Haynes and Jacqueline Gray of the IMS Survey Unit who had to deal with a major and complex activity. Susan Hayday provided valuable statistical and computing support to the study. The field work and interviews were carried out by Judith Harper and David Stevenson, together with Nigel Meager, James Hillage, Alan Anderson, Andrew Sanders, Hilary Metcalf, John Atkinson, Dick Waite, Richard Pearson and Amin Rajan who provided the sectoral analyses which provided the basis for this overall report. David Storey and Steve Johnson (Centre for Urban and Regional Studies) carried out the special small firms study. The overall project was directed by Amin Rajan and co-ordinated by Wendy Leigh who provided an excellent back-up support to the entire team from the outset.

This report was edited by Amin Rajan and Richard Pearson. The preparation of the manuscript was undertaken by Wendy Leigh, Amanda Tidey and Terry Page. Finally, the scale of the study was such that it could not be completed without the help and patience of the rest of the Institute's staff during the major activities of survey administration and report preparation.

Particular thanks must go to 4,000 companies, agencies and other bodies who provided valuable help and time, and often confidential data, without whose inputs this report would not be possible. The results of the study are, however, the responsibility of the IMS.

Summary

Introduction

This summary report presents the results of an employer-based study designed to identify the emerging occupational and employment trends over the period 1985-90, with particular reference to the underlying causes. The study was commissioned by the Occupations Study Group (OSG). They were concerned to identify the effect of recent changes in production methods, the use of new technologies and other factors on medium term employment trends in the UK. Their objective was to provide such information to policy makers in industry, education, Government and society, without offering any recommendations.

The study, carried out by the Institute of Manpower Studies (IMS), covers all types of employers in the economy - private and public, large and small. It excludes the 'black economy' and the voluntary sector. The study included in-depth in-company structured interviews with 450 employers; detailed questionnaires from 2,830 employers; an interview survey of 298 small firms; special studies covering agriculture and public services; discussions with 26 trade bodies; and use of secondary data sources. Between them, the employers interviewed and returning questionnaires employed eight million people, half the total workforce of the private sector and nationalised industries.

This information base, draws from employing organisations' plans and expectations along with their associated variabilities. Thus it is wide and varied, and provides a unique and detailed reference source about occupation and employment trends in the UK, as well as their underlying causes.

This summary focuses on four issues:

o   How is the workforce, and its sectoral distribution, expected to change over the period 1985-90, and why?

o   What kinds of jobs will be created, by whom, for whom, and why?

o   What will be the resulting occupational trends, and why?

o   What are perceived as key occupations for the future, and why?

The summary below draws on the main report which is in three parts. Part A provides the background to the study; Part B provides an assessment of the main employment trends and their underlying causes in the ten sectors of the economy, and in small firms; Part C brings together the main trends and developments affecting occupational and employment patterns across the whole economy up to 1990. Key occupations and skills are highlighted in the final Chapter.

Workforce and Sectoral Change to 1990, and the Underlying Causes

In 1985 the **production industries and agriculture** accounted for one third, and the **service industries** two thirds of the UK workforce. The largest service sector is distributive and financial and business services, with over six million jobs. The engineering and related industries constitute the largest production sector, with 2.5 million jobs.

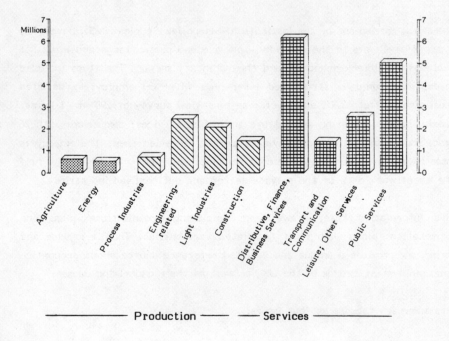

Figure 1   Sectoral Distribution - UK Workforce 1985

Organisations are changing their employment levels as a result of a complex interaction of market factors on the one hand; and changing technologies, working methods, production processes, and organisation structures, on the other. They are not able to quantify the relative impact of each of these factors on their employment or occupational elements.

Overall, the **production industries and agriculture** are expected to reduce their workforce by eight per cent, equivalent to about 665,000 jobs over the period 1985-90. Up to half of this decline will be due to organisations subcontracting activities to service sector employers. The **service industries** will increase their workforce by about 540,000 jobs, an overall increase of 3.6 per cent on their 1985 level. The net effect is that the overall workforce in the UK is expected to reduce by about 125,000 and total 23.58 million at the start of 1990. However, this forecast has a variability margin of +300,000 jobs.

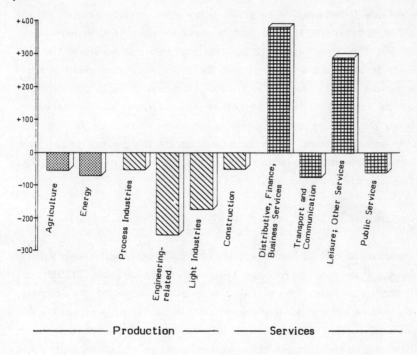

* These are mid point forecasts, the main report shows their variability.

Figure 2   Sectoral Change UK Workforce 1985-90

The major factors causing employment levels to fall across all the **production industries** are a combination of weak home demand, and insufficient international competitiveness. The latter is assisting import penetration and constraining exports. To improve competitiveness and productivity, employers are shedding uneconomic capacity and surplus labour; improving working methods and, particularly in the larger organisations, applying new technologies to both production and support activities. They are also increasing their subcontracting of production and services. The former is leading to the redistribution of jobs to small firms within the production industries; the latter to a growth in jobs in the service industries.

Employers in the production industries are expecting output to grow over the period to 1990. However, because of the factors cited above and consequent rising productivity, it will be jobless growth.

In the **service industries,** by contrast, significant employment growth is expected in distributive, financial and business services; and in leisure and other services. This growth is due to business expansion, primarily in the UK. They will be helped by subcontracting from the production industries and some other service sectors. Employment in transport and communication, however, is expected to fall, to either a reduction in over-capacity, or increasing competition. The latter is leading to the introduction of the new technologies and better working methods. Public sector employment is expected to fall, due to a combination of expenditure restraint, improved working methods, subcontracting and privatisation.

What Kind of Jobs Will Be Created, by Whom, for Whom, and Why?

Within these overall changes two categories of employment will grow by 1990. **Small firms** are expected to increase their workforce by about 700,000 jobs, many of them full-time. They will do this in every sector of the economy, except agriculture and energy. This growth will be partly organic, partly due to increased subcontracting by larger firms, and partly due to a competition-induced redistribution between organisations. For similar reasons, **self-employment** is also expected to grow by about 300,000.

A growing proportion of the new jobs will be **part-time,** particularly in medium and large service organisations with fluctuating workloads. The increasing standardisation and fragmentation of many service jobs supported by the application of new technologies will help promote part-time employment, which will rise from 21 per cent of total employment in 1985 to nearly a quarter by 1990.

The majority of the new jobs are expected to be filled by **female employees** for whom service sector and part-time working are expected to continue to be attractive. Overall their share of total employment is expected to rise from 45 per cent in 1985 to nearly half by 1990.

Organisations in all sectors expect to increase the proportion of **young people** (aged under 21) within their employment total. This is because they are perceived as more adaptable and trainable; the latter being assisted, in part, by the Youth Training Scheme.

What Will Be The Resulting Occupational Trends and Why?

Operatives form the largest occupational group across all the sectors. Otherwise the **production** and **service industries** have very different occupational structures. Craftsmen are the second largest group in the production industries; sales, clerical and personal service employees are the second largest group in the service sectors. Across all sectors, managers and professionals account for about 15 per cent of all staff.

The continuing shift from production to service-based industries will be a major influence on the changing occupational structure of the workforce. There will be at least three others: new technologies; weakening job demarcations; and organisational changes.

In the production industries growth is expected to favour skill- and knowledge-intensive occupations; particularly **engineers, scientists and technologists,** and multi-functional **craftsmen and technicians.** This is due to the growing use of new technologies; lessening job demarcations; and diversification into the selling of technical expertise.

In the services industries there will be significant growth in **personal and support service** occupations, mainly benefitting part-time staff. There will also be a smaller increase in the number of **professional** staff. This will reflect the expansion in the sector's output, some of which involves a redistribution of jobs from other sectors. In the public sector, **medical and welfare** related occupations are also expected to increase in line with an expansion in service provision.

The projected job gains in established **small firms** will favour the **less skill-intensive** occupations in both production and service activities. The projected job losses amongst larger employers are expected to involve mainly less skill-intensive occupations such as **operatives** and **clerical staff.** This will be due to reductions in surplus mannning, improved working methods, and the use of new technologies.

The overall change in the balance of occupations is shown below.

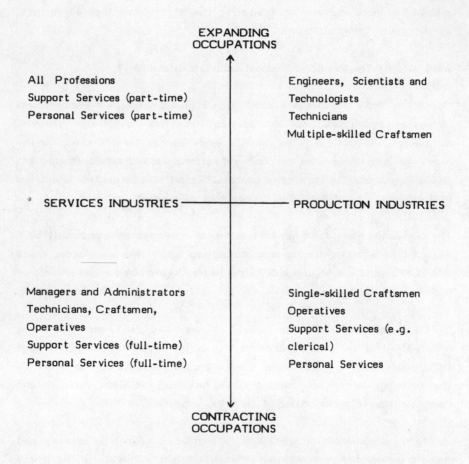

```
                          EXPANDING
                          OCCUPATIONS

                               ↑

All  Professions                        Engineers, Scientists and
Support Services (part-time)            Technologists
Personal Services (part-time)           Technicians
                                        Multiple-skilled Craftsmen



SERVICES INDUSTRIES ───────┼────── PRODUCTION INDUSTRIES




Managers and Administrators             Single-skilled Craftsmen
Technicians, Craftsmen,                 Operatives
Operatives                              Support Services (e.g.
Support Services (full-time)            clerical)
Personal Services (full-time)           Personal Services

                               ↓

                          CONTRACTING
                          OCCUPATIONS
```

Figure 3   The Changing Occupational Balance

What Will be the Key Occupations in the Future and Why?

Managers are seen to be vital to the future success of all types of organisation. Employers see a need to broaden managers' administrative, planning, commercial and human relations skills in order to achieve rising standards of performance.

The second important group are the **engineers, scientists and technologists,** principally in the production industries. Skill shortages are expected to continue to affect this group, and their numbers are expected to grow. This diverse group is increasingly expected to develop skills to apply information technology in all areas of work; to work across disciplines; and to develop project management and human relations skills.

Other professionals, particularly involved in data processing, accountancy and marketing, are also an important group in all types of organisation. They are needed to improve management functions and to improve the marketing of products and services.

A vital group in the production sector is **craftsmen and technicians;** they are increasingly expected to be multi-skilled in response to reducing job demarcations and to the greater use of the new technologies.

In the service industries, **personal and support service staff** in occupations such as retail sales assistants, bank cashiers and waiters are regarded as particularly important. They are increasingly required to develop broader based social, product, diagnostic and entrepreneurial skills to further the organisation's success.

Conclusion

Over the period to 1990 the size of the workforce is expected to remain broadly unchanged despite, rising output levels. However, there will be marked changes in its sectoral distribution: with a contraction in the production industries and expansion in the service industries. Within this overall assessment small firms and the self-employed will increase their share of the workforce. The number of part-time jobs will increase, particularly in personal and support services. The number of full-time jobs will decrease, particularly in the production industries.

More generally there will be a shift towards occupations with higher knowledge content and/or multiple skills. Across the economy, in all types of organisation, employers see the need to improve and broaden the skills of the workforce and increase their flexibility. This applies particularly to management and professional staff who are viewed as a key to business success in a changing market environment.

---

(1)   Rajan A, Pearson R (1986), UK Occupation and Employment Trends to 1990, Butterworths.

1 Introduction

The Study

The objective of this employer-based study is to determine the changing balance of employment and occupations in the UK over the period 1985-90, with particular reference to identifying the factors underlying these expected changes.

The study was originated by the Occupations Study Group (OSG). It was prompted by concern that since the middle of the last decade a number of changes have been taking place in production methods in response to the application of new technologies and other factors, and that the medium term impact of these changes on employment and occupations were unclear. While econometric models have been used to assess the changing employment patterns over a five year period using historical statistics, OSG felt that an employer-based study was better able to highlight both the underlying causes and the direction of change.

A feasibility study was undertaken by the Institute of Manpower Studies (IMS) to review what was known about these underlying changes, and to develop, if appropriate, a research methodology to identify the medium term employment and occupation trends and to provide insights into the underlying causal factors. The feasibility study highlighted the complexity of the issues involved in determining national employment trends, including the close inter-relationship between technological, organisational and economic factors. It also identified the extent to which employers were able and willing to provide detailed information on the subject. From that base, the methodology and objectives of this study were derived. This involved broadening the investigation to look beyond technological factors as underlying causes of change to embrace economic and organisational issues; as well as developing a classification scheme for broad occupational groups. The latter was necessary because of the

1

difficulty employers had in providing detailed occupational data against any nationally agreeable framework. Given the emphasis on trends and influences of an enduring nature, the study concentrates on the underlying causes and trends and not on short term, year by year fluctuations. Thus its focus is on employers' expectations of the medium term developments over the period to 1990.

Scope and Method

The study has three distinct dimensions: industrial, national and occupational. The information base has been devised to achieve a balanced representation of all the industries and economic regions of the UK. It also seeks to embrace all occupations within a realistic set of categories.

Its method of inquiry is entirely employer-based. It involved a research method with five elements. The first involved a nationwide postal survey, which yielded 2,830 detailed questionnaires from employers; this was followed by 450 structured in-depth in-company interviews which provided the basis for a series of detailed case studies. The former gave breadth to the information base, the latter the depth. The third element involved a special study, covering 298 company interviews in the small firms sector. A separate element involved analysis of developments in the public services and in agriculture. Finally, detailed discussions were held with representatives of trade bodies and an analysis made of appropriate secondary data sources. The main fieldwork for the study and the surveys was carried out during the second half of 1985.

Between them the employer-based interviews and questionnaires covered nearly eight million workers, half the workforce of the private sector and the nationalised industries. The special study of agriculture and the public services covered the full sectors. Thus the study has a credible base for assessing the various trends and their underlying effect on employment and occupations in the recent past and over the rest of the decade.

The Structure of the Report

The report's mode is to build up the assessment of the changing workforce from an analysis of the trends in each of the main sectors of the economy. This acts as a preliminary to constructing an aggregate picture. Accordingly, the report is in three parts.

Part A has two Chapters, concerned with background issues. They develop the rationale behind the study and the choice of methodology, the questions it covers and its mode of investigation. They also provide a basic snapshot of employment in the UK in 1985.

Part B details the changing employment patterns over the period to 1990, and underlying causal factors for individual sectors. In all, the UK employment structure is split into ten sectors: two covering primary activities, four manufacturing and construction activities, and four service activities. In view of their growing importance, a separate Chapter focuses on small firms.

Part C draws together the results from individual sectors and constructs an economy-wide picture in three Chapters. The first covers overall employment trends and the key compositional features of full and part-time work, as well as detailing the underlying causes of these changes. The next covers the occupational composition of the workforce in 1985 and highlights the main occupational trends in the national labour force over the period to 1990. The final Chapter draws together the data on what employers regard as key occupations and explains the way these occupations and their constituent skills are expected to change over the period to 1990.

A set of appendices provides more detailed statistical analyses of the results of the survey, questionnaires, discussion guide and background data.

Part A : Background

The background details of the study are drawn together in the following two Chapters.

Chapter 2 establishes the study's **raison d'etre;** the main argument being that the UK economy has undergone a number of fundamental changes in recent years that have been capable of altering the long term link between employment and output. Working methods are believed to be changing along with the occupational structure and its skills attributes. There is a need to study these developments in detail in order to make a realistic assessment of employment and occupational trends in the medium term to 1990. The developments are best studied at their point of impact - namely, the place of work; hence the need for an employer-based inquiry. Such an inquiry has an important merit. It can identify the qualitative and quantitative aspects of changes and their underlying causes at a micro level in a way that the standard mathematical models, through their reliance on historical statistical data sources, are not equipped to do.

Chapter 3 outlines the detailed features of the research method used. It also identifies the industrial and occupational dimensions of the study; and the issues explored along them. In the process, it develops the analytical base of the study and provides basic statistics on the UK workforce in 1985.

2 The Economic and Employment Context

Key Features of the Study

This study identifies the major trends and underlying factors identified by employers as affecting employment and its occupational elements in every sector of the economy over a five-year period to 1990. In two respects, it is different from other studies that have examined the UK's medium term employment prospects.

First and foremost, it is **employer-based.** It relies on an in-depth structured inquiry covering a cross section of individual employers in every size, activity and regional group in the economy. Unlike other studies, it makes no use of large scale mathematical models to derive future projections from modified or unmodified extrapolation of past trends.

Second, it concentrates on the **underlying trends** in employment rather than cyclical fluctuations around them, usually caused by policy and other changes at home and abroad. As such, its emphasis is on influences that are enduring and not subject to yearly changes. After all, from the point of view of planning and policy making in industry, education, Government, and society, it is the enduring influences that matter most. Shorter term changes are not, however, ignored. For example, the study does offer a tentative indication of the employment consequences of a sustained drop in oil prices.

The rest of this Chapter develops the arguments that underpin the adopted approach. Its main emphasis is on the rising importance of the enduring influences and the alternative methods of assessing them.

Ascendancy of Supply Side Changes

Since the late sixties, Western industrialised nations have been subjected to four 'supply-side' shocks - so called because they have progressively impinged on the prevailing methods of producing goods and services. In time sequence, they are the Kennedy Round of tariff reductions in 1968-70; the 1973 oil price increase; the 1979 oil price increase; and the information technology revolution, beginning in the middle of the last decade.

The tariff reductions unleashed new competitive forces in world trade hitherto subject to a number of controls introduced after the last war. For the UK these were soon reinforced by its entry into the EEC. No longer could domestic industry enjoy protection at home or in the privileged markets abroad. Even before this effect was evident, the first 'oil crisis' came. Not only did it inject an unprecedented deflationary bias into the world economy but it also initiated a concerted search for fuel saving technologies and more cost effective working methods. The process received a fresh impetus with the second 'oil crisis', in 1979, that brought in its wake the most severe output recession of this century.

The information technology revolution was born against the background of these developments. Isolated innovations in the separate areas of computing, electronics and telecommunications converged in the later part of the 1970s into the new information technology capable of application in every industrial and commercial activity, and affecting many occupations. Its potential for labour saving is due to its two principal attributes: automation and integration. Its capacity to capture, process, store and retrieve information can mechanise and integrate a number of hitherto labour intensive functions. Its technical interface with the established electrical, mechanical and hydraulic technologies can profoundly change the control aspects of both office and factory operations.

The first two supply-side shocks initiated changes in working methods and the long term relationships between output and employment. Their pace has been believed to be hastened by the second two, to the extent that forecasting employment with the conventional tools has become more uncertain.

A recent study covering the OECD countries showed that around two-thirds of the observed changes in labour productivity since 1974 can be attributed to the supply-side changes (Bruno, 1982; Bruno and Sach, 1982). In the UK

8

context, these changes have affected the utilisation and allocation of productive resources - both labour and capital. In the process, they have been reshaping conventional employment-output relationships in numerous industries in a way that has implications for their employment and occupational trends over the rest of this decade. Whether the recent fall in oil prices will have a reversing effect is too early to say in view of its extreme volatility. In any event, there are long time lags between the new price level once it is established and the full consequence of any changes in working methods.

But that does not detract from the point that the recent evolution of employment is unusual in the historical context. The changing level of employment is shown in Figure 2.1. This figure shows that aggregate employment has not recovered as in previous recoveries despite the fact that the current economic recovery has now been in progress for over four years - the longest recovery phase in the post-war history.

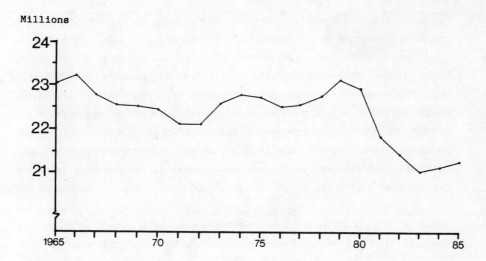

Source: Employment Gazette, March 1986

Figure 2.1   Evolution of Employment in the UK

9

Whatever the implications of the recent and earlier shocks, they can be studied either through an employer-based inquiry or an elaborate mathematical model. The two are not necessarily competitive; nor is either of them unambiguously superior to the other for all uses. The first constitutes a 'bottom-up' approach, starting as it does at the level of an individual employer, and then deriving inferences at the industry and then national level. The second one, in contrast, usually adopts a 'top-down' approach because it starts with developments and relationships at the macroeconomic level, and then derives inferences at the industry level. The level of detail available to the latter is highly dependent on the availability of regular and up-to-date statistics, which in the UK usually are only available in aggregate form. As such it is unable to provide a detailed understanding of causal factors. In the final analysis, the choice is largely influenced by the range of industries, the nature of employment-related issues, and the level of detail and understanding of underlying causes to be covered.

Why an Employer-Based Inquiry?

This study uses an employment-based inquiry for a three reasons. First and foremost, there is a need to identify more clearly the **nature** of past and prospective changes in the utilisation and allocation of labour and capital resources and their underlying causes. After all, an objective of this study is to go beyond the quantitative aspects of employment and highlight qualitative changes in skills and occupations in a way that gives policy makers in industry, education, Government and society a better appreciation of emerging manpower and training requirements. This clearly favours a bottom-up approach because its emphasis on individual employing organisations enables qualitative information about underlying causes to be picked up which a mathematical model, relying on secondary statistics, simply cannot provide.

Second, a model is not well suited to provide a detailed understanding of the effects of certain recent developments on employment in the medium term. 'New' developments such as technological or organisational innovations and the reform of The Wages Councils are not readily amenable to quantification. Moreover, a model's projections are usually influenced by relationships observed over a long period in the past. In so far as it can discount recent developments, this is done through a 'judgemental input' usually based on informed opinions on the part of the model builder. A more confined examination of such developments at the point of impact - namely, the

10

employment unit - is better placed to provide an early indication of emergent trends. This applies particularly to developments since 1979, occurring as they have in a very uncertain economic climate at home and abroad. Furthermore, this uncertainty makes it imperative to identify the characteristics of the leading-edge employers so that we know not only how the totality of jobs is changing, but also where the next generation of jobs will come from.

Finally, an employer-based inquiry is less exposed to ideological persuasion. For example, one of the main reasons behind the differences in the current forecasts of UK unemployment from different models relates to their respective economic perspectives. For example, the National Institute model, which is Keynesian in its orientation, predicts no major change in unemployment over the next two years (NIER, February 1986). In contrast, the monetarist-oriented Liverpool model predicts a notable fall (Liverpool Quarterly Economic Bulletin, March 1986). Both use the same data in estimating the underlying relationships between unemployment and other variables. Where they differ is in their assessment of the success of the economic policy. This is not to belittle the usefulness of these models but merely to labour the point that the model-based projections are not incontrovertible. On the other hand, the employer-based projections enable one to examine the circumstances of individual firms closely enough to draw out employers' expectations and practices and thus minimise the risk of value judgement by the researchers.

That said, it is worth highlighting the limitations of the employer-based inquiry. The obvious one is that many employers do not have well formulated five-year employment plans. Also, where plans exist, they are not immutable. They are usually conditional on expectations about critical factors such as market trends and shares, new technologies, changing working methods and economic outlook. Finally, even within a single organisation it is possible to uncover differing perceptions on its employment outlook. These limitations were well recognised at the outset. However, in mitigation a number of observations can be made, each being borne out by the elaborate feasibility study (described in the next Chapter) which preceded this study.

The main observation relates to the unexpected ferocity of the last recession and the sheer scale of the enforced labour shake-out that followed. This has vastly heightened the need for manpower planning in every sector of the economy. Whereas day-to-day recruitment matters may be left to the managers, organisational boards are increasingly treating manpower as an essential element of corporate plans in the medium term. Manpower implications of strategic decisions are now more regularly appraised and aligned with overall corporate objectives. The feasibility study apart, this message is coming through clearly from the diverse range of employer-based projects undertaken at the IMS since 1980. Furthermore, in so far as organisations have no manpower plans because of uncertainty, the employer-based inquiry serves to highlight this as well as the factors responsible. Again, from the policy makers' point of view, it is useful to know the industrial dimension of uncertainty rather than have it shrouded under an aggregation procedure, as is the case with mathematical models.

Finally, as we show in the next Chapter, the inquiry specifically precludes an opinion poll type off-the-cuff response as far as possible. In each case, the inquiry not only covers the current and prospective employment trends but most importantly seeks out the underlying causal factors. Thus, all along in the report, trends are viewed within a clear and consistent causative framework: analysis of performance and change receives as much, if not more, prominence as the trends themselves. Beyond that, the report also highlights the variabilities around the trends consistent with the alternative evolution of the causal factors in the medium term. At the level of the individual employing organisation, where inconsistencies have been apparent between employment prospects and causal factors, these have been resolved as far as possible through further consultations. Also, where inconsistencies have emerged between firms - like every firm within an industry expecting to increase its market share - this has been corrected when individual projections are aggregated and grossed up for the industry.

3 Scope and Research Method

Scope

The coverage of this employer-based study, which includes all the regions of
the UK, is defined along two dimensions: industrial and occupational. It
covers the entire workforce - defined as employment plus self-employment -
engaged in paid work and excludes voluntary working and the 'Black Economy'.

In order to disaggregate the national picture into industries and sectors,
reference is made to the official 1980 Standard Industrial Classification
(SIC) which is used to codify and structure national industrial and employment
statistics. In the first instance, all data collection and analysis for the
study is done at the level of 55 individual classes. In this report, however,
the results are presented in a more aggregated form in order to facilitate
presentation as well as to conceal the identity of individual employers. The
latter consideration is important: in the face of growing industrial
concentration, employment in a number of industrial classes is dominated by
large oligopolies. Their participation in this study could only be secured
through an undertaking to observe a strict anonymity.

Accordingly, the analysis is focused in ten main **sectors.** These are shown in
Table 3.1 along with their share in total employment (see also Figure 3.1) and
national output. In each case, the composition is influenced by one of two
considerations: overlap in the nature of activities and similarity in the
market environment. For example, distributive, financial and business services
are amalgamated because of the growing similarity in the nature of their
respective businesses resulting from competitive diversification. Similarly,
all publicly provided services have been combined because they are not
marketed and the level of expenditure and employment is largely determined by
a single organisation, the Government. In all cases, the grouping
substantially follows the logical sequence as set out in the 1980 SIC
nomenclature.

Table 3.1   Industrial Sectors* and Their Role in the National Economy 1985

Sector:	Percentage Share of National		
	Output**	Employment	Self-Employment
Primary Industries			
(1) Agriculture, Forestry, Fishing	3	2	12
(2) Energy and Water Supply	10	3	na
Manufacturing			
(3) Process Industries	7	4	na
(4) Engineering and Related Industries	12	12	na
(5) Light Production Industries	12	10	na
Construction			
(6) Construction and Allied Industries	7	4	20
Services			
(7) Distributive, Financial and Business Services	21	24	44
(8) Transport and Communication	7	6	4
(9) Leisure and Related Services	na	11	20
(10) Public Services	na	24	na

na = not available or applicable

*   See Appendix A.5 for the coverage of each sector in terms of the 1980
     Standard Industrial Classification. Later in the report, references are
     made to 'production industries' and 'marketed services'. The former
     comprises sectors 2-6; and the latter, sectors 7-9.

**   22 per cent is not allocated on an industrial basis because of data
     unavailability.

Source: CSO Commodity Flow Accounts (1985); Employment Gazette (March 1986);
        Annual Review of Agriculture.

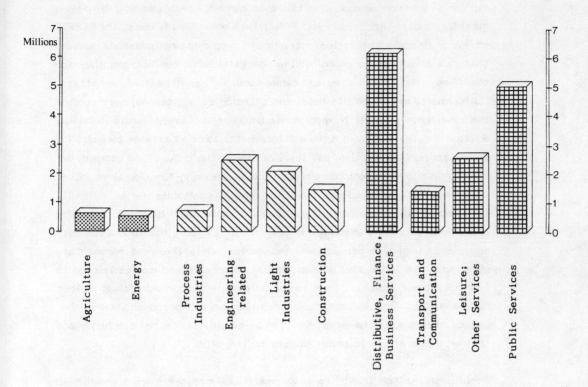

Source: Employment Gazette

Figure 3.1   Sectoral Workforce: 1985

15

In contrast, the **occupational** dimension is not directly patterned over a set nomenclature, because the available nomenclatures, such as the official Classification of Occupations and Directory of Occupational Titles (CODOT), call for an enormous amount of detail that can only be attempted through a mandatory inquiry like the ten-year Population Census. In any event, the CODOT scheme or its variants have less relevance in employing organisations because their data on occupations do not follow any established conventions: they are based on job titles in some cases, and on qualifications in others. Furthermore, industries like hotel and catering or engineering have evolved their own nomenclatures to meet their unique requirements while individual employers collect data in different forms: for some it relates to skill, for others qualification, function, pay level or bargaining group. One company we saw had over 250 different job titles in the engineering function alone. Even collecting detailed occupational data from similar companies can be difficult. For example, the Engineering Industry Training Board which has been collecting occupational data from engineering employers for 20 years has to ask for data aggregated into nine occupational categories, while the most recent data collected by the Hotel and Catering Industry Training Board was restricted to four occupational groupings. These cannot be readily reconciled with any other national system. The task being faced was to devise a **compromise** scheme that broadly conformed to the definitions used by employers, on the one hand; and that would be of use to policy makers on the other.

Accordingly, in the feasibility study nearly 350 employers were approached together with their trade associations across all industrial sectors to test the methodology and to develop an occupational framework. From it emerged two schemes - one for production-related activities and one for services - summarised in Table 3.2 and described in detail in the questionnaires in Appendix A.1 and A.2. Ideally we would have liked to collect more detailed occupational data. In practice, however, it was clear that many employers would not be able to provide more detail. The main consideration, therefore, was to derive data sets that were consistent across industrial sectors.

Both schemes put more emphasis on functions performed by job holders and less on formal qualifications. The two attributes are, of course, not unrelated. For professional and knowledge-based occupations, they are highly correlated but as one moves down the occupational hierarchy the link becomes weaker. The feasibility study suggested that for nearly 70 per cent of the employees the nature of work rather than its educational attributes best defined the occupations.

Table 3.2   Occupational Groups Used in the Study

Production Sector	Service Sector
(a) Managers and Administrators	(a) Managers and Administrators
(b) Engineers, Scientists and Technologists	(b) All Professions
(c) Other Professions	: scientific
	: others
(d) Technicians and Draftsmen	
(e) Craftsmen	(c) Support Services
: foremen and supervisors	: clerical
: engineering	: sales
: transferable	
: non-transferable	(d) Personal Service Occupations
	: security
(f) Operatives	: personal service
: skilled	(e) Technicians, Craftsmen and Operatives
: others	: technicians
	: craftsmen
(g) Support Services	: operatives
: clerical	
: sales	(f) Others
(h) Personal Service Occupations	
: security	
: personal service	
(i) Others	

Source: Appendix A.1 and A.2

Given the study's emphasis on the skill requirements of the emergent employment trends, it seemed more sensible to put greater weight on the first attribute, especially for the non-professional occupations.

Finally, although the study embraces all the standard economic regions of the UK, a detailed regional analysis has not proved possible. Although the sampling base has been devised specifically to cover establishments, a number of major participants - particularly in the service sectors - operate multiple branches across different regions, and were only able to code their responses under the principal region of activity. As such, regions with a high proportion of 'branch' plants or establishments may appear to have a lower employment coverage than would seem to be the case. A region-by-region assessment would therefore be somewhat arbitrary.

Research Method - The Feasibility Study

The research method seeks to obtain information on recent and prospective employment trends from employers in every sector. Given the diversity in employer size outside the public sector, this involved both small firms, single establishments of large firms and large firms in totality. In this context, the focus of the study has to be the unit or the level where the medium term employment targets are planned and monitored. In practice, this is far from easy. In view of the centralised control of manning levels in many firms this can involve looking at not just a single establishment but the whole firm where corporate plans are designed and monitored. This diversity counsels a more comprehensive and varied approach.

Accordingly, the one adopted here has a number of strands. Together, they are designed to serve two objectives: to cover the main employers in each SIC class and to secure a cross section of the remaining employers. The underlying objective is to capture both a high employment coverage and diversity. The approach has four elements: a postal survey; case studies; clustered studies; and special studies. The main fieldwork of the study was carried out in the second half of 1985.

Before outlining the detailed features, it is worth spelling out the results of a **feasibility study** which served to shape them. A six month long exercise was carried out in the second half of 1984; it involved four distinct activities.

First, a basic desk review was undertaken of existing employment studies and databases to explore potential methodologies and draw out the lessons for this study. One of the objectives was to identify the best available listing, or register, of employers in the UK to be used as a basis for constructing a representative cross sectional sample of employers. As the IMS has been involved in such studies since 1970, there was a wealth of experience already on hand. Nevertheless, extensive discussions were held with other researchers both in the academic community and in consultancies, as well as with the staff in trade bodies, government departments and agencies. We were also able to draw off the experience of researchers and organisations overseas who had attempted similar studies. From this work a structure for the pilot survey was developed, including draft questionnaires and interview schedules.

The second involved a trial postal survey to test the reliability and currency of the directories of employers in different industries and the ability and likelihood of employers providing the necessary data. The questionnaire was comprehensive: it provided an indication of the validity (or otherwise) of the proposed questions. The results helped to improve the sample base and the questionnaire design. The feedback on occupational groups was particularly helpful.

The third involved structured face-to-face, in-company interviews, with threefold objectives: to identify the nature of the key employment-related issues in different industries; to ascertain whether the participants in fact had considered plans or views on their own organisations' employment evolution in the medium term; and finally to confirm whether employers would be willing to divulge confidential company data to the research team. This activity provided valuable insights into the main determinants of employment and the best approach to them at the company level.

The fourth activity involved extensive consultations with more than twenty main sectoral associations across the whole economy as listed in Appendix A.4. They proved particularly helpful in identifying large and/or leading-edge employers, key factors affecting employment, previous studies and main data sources.

The feasibility study thus helped shape the survey design, theme issues and all the background information in a structured way. The questionnaires resulting from it and used in the main postal survey are given at Appendix A.1 and A.2; and the discussion guide for case studies at Appendix A.3.

Methodological points aside, the feasibility study also suggested four **subject areas** worthy of special attention: small firms; self-employment; inward investment; and corporate mergers and takeovers. They are special in the sense that their relevance is not sector-specific but cuts across the whole of the private sector. Although highly topical, there was felt to be a dearth of information about their employment effects and their assessment would require a rather different methodology. So much for the feasibility study. The four elements of the research method are now considered individually below and then brought together.

The Postal Survey

The sample of employers used was drawn from two sources: the databases of Market Location Limited and Dunn and Bradstreet Limited. The former proved to be a good source for manufacturing, extractive and construction activities; and the latter for services. Each has the details of over 150,000 employers in its respective database.

From these was drawn a cross-sectional sample of 6,488 employing organisations, at establishment level as far as possible. When drawing the sample, care was taken to ensure that its employment-size, industrial and regional characteristics were representative of the overall corporate population to the extent that the latter's detailed features were known. In this respect, significance was attached to information emerging from the latest (1984) Annual Census of Production, save in one sense. The Census has a highly skewed distribution, with only two per cent of the manufacturing establishments having over 1,000 employees. The sample developed for the survey has nearly 15 per cent. This was deliberate in order partly to guard against the possibility of a low response rate in this group and partly to secure a big enough base for each employment-size group to permit realistic generalisations.

The Chief Executive of each of the sampled organisations was approached via a letter from the Chairman and Trustees of the OSG, and asked to complete the detailed questionnaire. Non-respondents were reminded by telephone and sent up to three reminders. Table 3.3 gives the response pattern. It prompts two points: that the overall response rate at 55 per cent is highly satisfactory for a large non mandatory inquiry like this; and the survey produced a database of 2,830 respondents (hereafter known as **'The IMS/OSG Survey'**). This figure excludes around 700 returns that were not usable for three reasons.

About 400 applied to organisations that had ceased to exist as original entities, due to corporate mergers or outright deaths. The remaining 300 either gave insufficient information, or had the information but would not divulge it for reasons of commercial confidentiality.

The study also achieved a satisfactory coverage of the employment-size groups and regions. Appendices A.6 to A.7 provide the disaggregated details. The high response rate was achieved with the active co-operation and help of the staff of Business in Community, embracing the nationwide network of enterprise agencies. Their local staff answered queries on the study and the survey questions from participants in their localities and were able to identify companies that had ceased trading.

Table 3.3   Survey Response Rate

| Sectors | Number of Organisations: | | | Number of Usable Returns |
	Approached (a)	Replied (b)	Response Rate (a - b) 100	
Manufacturing, Extractive and Construction Industries	3,564	1,865	53	1,599
Service Industries	2,924	1,674	57	1,231
Total	6,488	3,539	55	2,830

Source: IMS/OSG Survey

The Case Studies

On the basis of structured in-company interviews, 450 case studies were constructed, using a detailed discussion guide. They involved two distinct groups of employers: a selection of 255 respondents from the postal survey; and 195 of the largest employers, drawn from each sector outside the public services. Over 80 per cent of the companies approached for an interview cooperated and supplied detailed information. The approach to companies was made via an introductory letter from the Chairman of the OSG to the Chairman or Chief Executive, who often participated in the interviews. Otherwise the interviews were normally undertaken with board level representatives of corporate planning and personnel, their specialist staffs, and line and technical managers.

The **survey group** comprised a cross section within each SIC class, representing each employment size band and region. The survey respondents were included in the case studies for two reasons: to validate the questionnaire response through a more detailed inquiry and to obtain a more detailed perspective of past and prospective developments. Whilst the postal survey provided the breadth in industrial, occupational and regional terms, the follow-up case studies were devised to provide the depth in subject terms.

The **large employer group**, in contrast, covered major national companies and groups - both UK and foreign-owned, and often operating in more than one sector - as well as the nationalised industries. Their employment size apart, the main reason for including them in the case studies was that they often have a key employment perspective at the corporate level. Their manpower targets are increasingly aligned to other strategic objectives; so that it makes sense to examine the totality of their position. In a number of them, the determination of overall employment levels and manpower planning was done centrally. In so far as planning was devolved to the subsidiaries, the latter filed separate returns wherever possible. However, very detailed information could not always be supplied for the 'bottom line' subsidiaries. For example, one conglomerate had 15 divisions controlling, in turn, 450 subsidiaries in four sectors with a total headcount of over 100,000. Here, much useful information was provided but only at the divisional level.

The sample for the 195 largest employers was compiled from THE TIMES 1000 list of companies (1984-85 edition). They were chosen primarily on the basis of their principal activities, in order to ensure that large employers in each SIC class were included. Their **proximate** distribution between the sectors is given in Table 3.4, by both principal and spillover activities - the latter resulting from their conglomerate nature.

Two sectors were particularly affected by spillover activities: construction and leisure and related services. Due to increasing vertical integration, the former is closely linked with some of the heavy production industries (like engineering) and the latter with light production industries (like food, drink and tobacco). The overall distribution is therefore indicative of the spread

of activities covered by the THE TIMES 1000 group here; even though its
principal activities are well defined.

Table 3.4   Sectoral Distribution of Case Study Employers

| Sector: | Number of Organisations | | Spillover Activity Of Times 1000 Organisations* |
	Survey	Large Employers - Times 1000	
1. Agriculture, Forestry, Fishing	1	2	5,7
2. Energy and Water Supply	6	16	3,4,7
3. Process Industries	42	21	2,4
4. Engineering and Related Industries	51	35	3,5,6,7,8
5. Light Production Industries	48	37	4,7,8,9
6. Construction	21	9	4,7
7. Distributive, Financial and Business Services	26	41	5,8,9
8. Transport and Communication	13	21	7
9. Leisure and Related Services	47	13	2,5,7
Total	255	195	

* This indicates the degree of overlap between the main sectors by the
largest employers

Source: IMS/OSG Survey and Case Studies

Cluster Studies

The **cluster studies,** forming the third strand of the research method
concentrated on three sets of activity: agriculture, forestry and fishing;
financial services; and public services.

The approach to the first of these was dictated by the fact that it is dominated by small farmers and it would not be appropriate to cover sectoral developments via a postal survey. Discussions with their trade body suggested a two-pronged approach that relied on case studies and expert opinion on the one hand; and secondary data sources on the other.

The second activity - financial services - had recently been covered in detail at the IMS in a parallel study (Rajan, 1985). Its aims and research methods are directly related to those of this study. Given its newness, its general conclusions are also relevant. For this sector, however, case studies interviews updated the detailed findings and also assessed prospective developments, including the 'Big Bang' in the securities markets; the proposed de-regulation of the building societies; and the Budgetary changes affecting life insurance.

The third activity - public services - is best covered separately because ultimately it involves a single body, the Government, setting cash limits and thus directing or influencing manpower budgets. Here again, a two-pronged approach was adopted: reference to employment plans in the latest Government Expenditure Plans (Cmnd 9702-1), on the one hand, and detailed discussions with Central and Local Government departments and health authorities, on the other, to obtain a more detailed occupational perspective.

Special Studies

Special studies formed the final strand of the research methodology. As mentioned earlier, the feasibility study identified four subject areas - mergers/takeovers, inward investment, self-employment and very small firms - for special attention. They cut across all the sectors, with the exception of public services. Each was viewed as having a potentially important effect on the evolution of employment and warranted special investigation. Accordingly, where relevant, the first two were given prominence in the interviews underpinning the case studies. In addition, the case studies took special account of employers, future plans regarding acquisitions and divestments when considering employment change in order to avoid 'double counting'. The second also involved a detailed analysis of secondary sources. The self-employed were covered in part in the small firms study (described below) and in part via those employers in our case studies who contracted the services of the self-employed. In addition, recourse was made to secondary sources to derive the overall estimates for changes in self-employment, duly taking into account their known limitations.

Small firms were covered through a separate detailed study which involved 298 small firms in six localities. This was carried out by Dr David Storey and Stephen Johnson at the Centre for Urban and Regional Development Studies at Newcastle University in conjunction with the IMS. The study involved detailed interviews in six highly differentiated labour markets with 50 small firms in each locality. The underlying objective was to examine the employment prospects and occupational structures of small firms in diverse settings in order to have a clearer appreciation of the role of the market environment and local industrial structure. The following labour markets were covered:

London	:	a capital city, with a strong service sector;
Glasgow	:	a provincial conurbation with a varied manufacturing base;
Reading	:	a growing sub-dominant 'city' with a high-tech sector;
Morecambe/ Lancaster	:	a free standing town with tourist and light industries;
Cleveland	:	a declining manufacturing area;
Corby	:	in the Midlands with an active policy for small firms.

Between them, the 298 firms covered every activity. The separate survey that covered them is hereafter referred to as the IMS/OSG Small Firms Survey. Their distribution between sectors is outlined in Chapter 14. It was influenced partly by the industrial structure of the chosen labour markets and partly by their overall distribution in the economy.

In addition, an extensive literature review and assessment of previous research on small firms was undertaken.

Employment Coverage

Now that the individual strands of the research method have been covered, this section brings together the first three to show the number of employees covered in each sector through the different strands. This is given in Table 3.5. The fourth strand is excluded because it is subject, and not industry, specific.

Table 3.5   Employment Coverage

Sector:	Employment Coverage				
	(a)	(b)	(c)	(d)=(a+b+c)	(e)
	IMS/OSG Postal Survey	Times 1000 Group Case Studies	Cluster Studies	Total Employment Coverage	Employment in 1985*
	'000	'000	'000	'000	'000
Primary Industries					
1. Agriculture, Forestry, Fishing	-	(64)	364	364	364
2. Energy and Water Supply	26	702**	-	728	596
Manufacturing					
3. Process Industries	207	547	-	754	779
4. Engineering and Related Industries	569	1,014	-	1,583	2,549
5. Light Production Industries	434	930	-	1,364	2,042
6. Construction	46	236	-	282	933
Services					
7. Distributive, Financial and Business Services	569	758	498	1,825	5,049
8. Transport and Communication	315	747	-	1,062	1,266
9. Leisure and Related Services	339	333	-	672	2,196
10. Public Services	-	-	5,010	5,010	5,010
Total	2,505	5,267	5,872	13,644	20,784

* Excludes self-employment

** Includes employment of other sectors because of the multi-sectoral coverage of certain oil companies and nationalised industries.

Sources: (a), (b) and (c) as mentioned above (e) from **Employment Gazette,** February 1986

The two main strands of the study - postal survey and case studies - have covered 6.8 million employees in the private sector and 1 million in nationalised industries; equivalent to half of their total employment. This is a slight over-estimate because the totals in column (e) relate to Great Britain whereas those in columns (a) and (b) also cover Northern Ireland. When appropriate allowance is made, the overall coverage is about 49 per cent.

To conclude this Chapter, four points need emphasis. First, the coverage for agriculture and the public services is high because of the cluster approach. Second, the coverage outside these sectors is indicative and not definitive, in view of the spillover activities of the conglomerates. Even so, the employment coverage is high by the standard of a non-mandatory inquiry.

Third, the main strands of the method are the postal survey and the case studies. The underlying objective has been to devise a sampling base that has the maximum employment coverage as well as the inter-firm or inter-establishment diversity within it. The 55 per cent response rate for the postal survey is satisfactory, as is the overall employment coverage. Together, they provide a credible base for making an assessment of the current and prospective trends in employment, its occupational elements and the underlying causes of change.

Finally, the central objective of the research is to identify the trends in employment and occupations as well as their underlying causes. Any forecasting exercise has to have a margin of uncertainty. The estimates presented in this report are, therefore, accompanied by a variability margin that account for unavoidable errors in deriving the numbers as well as in the assessment of the relative importance of various influences.

Part B : Individual Sectors

This part reports on the ten individual sectors comprising the total UK employment, together with the special analysis of small firms which cross all sectors.

Each Chapter covers the following topics for the appropriate sector:

(i)   its role in the national economy and recent workforce trends;

(ii)   the underlying causes of these trends;

(iii)   the factors expected to influence the sector's workforce in the period to 1990, its size, and the possible variabilities in the forecast;

The first topic draws on the discussions with the sectoral bodies and analysis of secondary sources; the latter two are based on those of the 450 case study interviews and 2,830 questionnaires relevant to the sector. It should be noted that the tables from the **IMS/OSG Survey** do not include the responses from the 'large employer' case studies. The number of survey respondents in each sector are given in Appendix A.5. The assessments of future workforce levels emerging from the survey and the case studies were based on the participants own assessments of the economic outlook. They broadly envisaged that economic growth would average around two to three per cent per annum, a figure consistent with prevailing conditions.

In three important aspects - occupations; full and part-time employment; age and sex composition - there is considerable inter-sectoral commonality in the results. Where there are strong sectoral features, these are highlighted in the relevant sectoral Chapters. Otherwise, the topics are treated under separate headings in the three Chapters in Part C. As such, Part B concentrates on the quantitative aspects of employment, while Part C concentrates on its qualitative aspects, some common themes and a comparison with other forecasts.

There is one more omission in Part B. Each Chapter in it applies to Great Britain because comparable data series for Northern Ireland are not available. However, once the estimates for Great Britain are duly aggregated and converted on the same basis as those of Northern Ireland, the UK estimates are derived. This is done in Part C.

In deriving the future trends in workforce, particular attention has been paid to the forecasting **methods** used by the study's participants. The validity and limitations of the methods, as well as their possible error margins, have been taken into account when aggregating the individual participant organisations' forecasts to derive the industry-wide forecasts. The procedure also takes into account:

(i)   the employment size of each participant organisation;

(ii)   how realistic its expectations of its industry's business prospects are in the light of the current market penetration rates and the medium term prospects of the UK and world economy;

(iii)   the validity of its expectations of its own market share in relation to its competitors' expectations of market shares; and

(iv)   whether future growth in employment will be organic or acquisitional; if the latter, allowance has been made to avoid the possible double-counting.

As for **presentation,** the objective of the study is to focus on economy-wide developments. To do this it was necessary to develop a series of detailed sectoral profiles. The Chapters in this part of the report provide a broad overview of the main trends in the sectors.

Finally, the historic data presented are given for different cyclical years in order to compare similar cyclical points when identifying the underlying trends. In this context, the cyclical turning points are identified from the Central Statistical Office's index of cyclical indicators. These show the following trough and peak years for the cyclical phases since 1970 in the UK economy:

Trough Years	Peak Years	Cyclical Phases	Nature of Phases
1971	1973	1971-73	Upswing
		1973-75	Downswing
1975	1979	1975-79	Upswing
		1979-81	Downswing
1981	1985 (latest)	1981-85	Upswing

Source: Economic Trends (various issues)

4 Agriculture, Forestry and Fishing

Background

This sector covers three distinct industries noted for their high natural resource intensity. Of the three, agriculture is the largest, irrespective of the measure of size used (Table 4.1) . It is also the one which has undergone the most substantive changes in the last 15 years responding to national and EEC policies. In terms of national output, employment and foreign trade the sector's role is relatively low (Table 3.1; Appendix B.1 and B.2) . It does, however, account for about one in eight of national self-employment. Strategically, it is also very important, providing over 60 per cent of national food needs. As explained in Chapter 3, the analyses for this sector draw heavily off interviews with sectoral experts and secondary sources. The Chapter details the main trends in the sector.

Table 4.1   Employment and Self-Employment in Agriculture, Forestry and Fishing: 1985

(thousands)

		1985
Agriculture+	Regular Full-time	165
	Regular Part-time	61
	Seasonal/Casual	99
	Self-employed*	291
	Total	616
Forestry		17
Fishing		22
	Sectoral Total	655

+   UK Figures for Agriculture

*   This is the category 'farmers, partners and directors', which approximates to 'self-employment' in the Annual Review of Agriculture .

Source: Annual Review of Agriculture and Employment Gazette, February 1986

Table 4.2   Agriculture: Evolution of UK Workforce 1971-85

(thousands)

Components of Workforce	1971 (Trough)	1973 (Peak)	1975 (Trough)	1979 (Peak)	1981 (Trough)	1985 (Latest Peak)
(a) Employees:						
Hired Workers		238	220	196	182	162
Family Workers	418	94	83	55	55	56
Seasonal/Casual Workers	na	78	73	97	97	99
Salaried Managers	na	6	7	8	8	8
(Sub-total)	(418)	(416)	(383)	(356)	(342)	(325)
(b) Farmers, Partners & Directors (Self-Employed)	298	288	280	304	294	291
Total Workforce	716	704	663	660	636	616

na = not available

Source: Annual Review of Agriculture (various issues)

An examination of past trends in the agriculture workforce in Table 4.2 prompts three points. First, the size of the workforce shows little cyclical sensitivity: both employment and self-employment register a secular long term downward trend. Second, there are clear compositional changes, improving the relative position of two distinct groups: seasonal and casual workers; and the self-employed, covering farmers, partners and directors. Third, this compositional shift is indicative of changes occurring in three areas: size distribution of employing units; status composition; and training.

Currently, employment is highly concentrated in a few large agricultural holdings. According to the 1984 Wages Inquiry, 64 per cent of holdings in England and Wales had no regular employees; 11 per cent employed only seasonal workers; and four per cent employed only part-timers. Amongst the remaining 21 per cent, about a half had only one regular full-time hired employee. In terms of female employees, the industry is clearly evading the national trend as the share of females in overall employment is falling (Annual Review of Agriculture) although the part-time numbers are increasing both for males and females.

In terms of the occupational balance and skill content of work, there is indirect evidence that the skill content has increased. As Table 4.3 shows, the share of managerial and craft-based occupations has increased, while that of operatives - covering cowmen, drivers and farm workers - has decreased. This is further corroborated by the data from the Agriculture Training Board: in 1965-66, only one per cent of the regular workforce received formal training. By 1982-83 this had risen to nearly 50 per cent. This training has been confined mainly to managerial, supervisory and craft occupations although more operatives are now receiving formal training. Thus it is clear that the human capital component of the workforce has been increasing, alongside the secular decline in its numerical size.

Table 4.3   Occupational Composition of Hired Full-Time Men in Agriculture: 1978-84

                                                        (percentages)

Grades (Occupations):	1978	1984
Grade 1 (Managers)	2.6	3.6
Grade 2 (Supervisors and Foremen)	6.1	6.2
Craftsmen (all disciplines)	26.4	27.4
Ordinary (Operatives and Others)	64.9	62.9
Total	100	100

Source: Ministry of Agriculture, Fisheries and Food

The workforce in **forestry** has been contracting at the rate of 2.5 per cent per annum since the middle of the last decade to around 17,000 in 1985. Much of the decline is in the public sector which is the largest employer in this industry. In **fishing** too, the workforce has seen a decline; but a very small one from a level of 22,000 since the late seventies. There has also been a trend towards greater part-time as opposed to full-time employment.

Workforce Trends and Their Causes to 1985

A notable feature of the long term decline in the sector's workforce is that it has occurred against the background of rising output (Table 4.4). The implication is that labour productivity has increased - in the peak and the trough years in the economy.

The causes of this increased productivity are two fold and inter-related. The growth in output has been directly assisted by the price support system under the Common Agriculture Policy (CAP) of the EEC. Indirectly, however, it has generated a knock-on effect on production methods, aided and abetted by energy price rises.

Table 4.4   Agriculture Output, Workforce and Productivity 1971-85

(Annual Average Percentages)

Time Periods:	(a) Growth in Output	(b) Growth in Workforce	(c) = (a) - (b) Implied Growth in Productivity
Trough Years 1971-75	0.1	-1.9	2.0
Peak Years 1973-79	1.1	-1.0	2.1
Trough Years 1975-79	4.5	-0.7	5.2
Peak Years 1979-85	5.3	-1.2	6.5

Source: CSO Annual Output Series; Annual Review of Agriculture (various years)

This effect has been manifested through two developments: agglomeration and innovation. Through the former, the average size of agricultural holding has increased. The inherent bias towards increased production in the CAP provisions has promoted restructuring in order to achieve the economies of scale. This in turn has favoured innovations, in farming techniques as well as physical structures such as buildings and equipment. The former have assisted in the development of new 'products' in the form of new strains of crops and livestock. As such, they have relied on disembodied technical progress, with innovations coming through the increased knowledge content of the intensive farming techniques. Innovations have equally come in the embodied form, through the acquisition of more modern equipment and information technologies. Conventional mechanical and hydraulic technologies apart, the industry has begun to use computer-based devices in, for example, portable instrumentation, sorting, analysis and office equipment. The scale of usage to date, however, is small.

In forestry and fishing, too, labour saving methods have been used. These include a more efficient system of planting, felling and transporting trees; as well as in processing the fish catch.

These labour saving devices were applied at a time when higher industrial earnings were encouraging a migration out of agriculture. With rising unemployment elsewhere in this decade, however, the 'pull' factor has weakened somewhat. In any event, this was a minor factor even in the last decade when compared to the 'industrialisation' of the sector speeded up by the CAP. This process has affected not only the quantity but also the quality of work, making for greater differentiation in the occupational structure.

Workforce Trends and Their Causes 1985-90

Looking to the future, the nature of these influences is unlikely to change. But the same cannot be said about their direction.

In agriculture the thrust of the CAP is unmistakably changing towards ending the persistent over-production hitherto generated by generous price support. The clearest indication of it came with the imposition of milk quotas in1984. Earlier this year a three-point crisis package was proposed: a £1.8 billion subsidy to sell surpluses in the world markets; a freeze on price guarantees; and specific disincentives on surplus production of specific commodities. The CAP is expected to continue to become more restrictive in its support for agriculture. What is not clear, however, is the time span of the impending reforms and their ultimate shape.

In this context, the projections of employment assume gradual changes in the CAP. Their precise nature cannot be identified; but their thrust will intensify the squeeze on farm incomes, already under severe pressure since at least the beginning of this decade (see the Annual Review of Agriculture, 1985). In its wake will come four developments, already apparent in recent figures.

First, the increase in the shares of self-employment, family labour and casual work will continue, if not intensify. Second, reductions in food prices will affect land values which have hitherto enjoyed speculative appeal amongst institutional investors. This is expected to encourage diversification into land-based 'self-service' activities like camping and recreation. Third, the trend towards agglomeration will ease; partly because its economics will be severely undermined without the CAP support, and partly because many farms have reached an optimal size. Fourth, the pace of innovation will slacken because lower incomes will reduce the rate of return on capital and non-labour inputs - both of which are subject to regular inflationary increases. Furthermore, there is now greater awareness of the detrimental environmental effects of intensive farming based on high chemical and energy usage.

In **forestry,** there are three factors which will affect the underlying trend in employment: demand, technology and the declining role of the public sector. Home demand is set to remain high; so is production, which is expected to increase by about six per cent per annum till 1990, as trees planted after the last war reach maturity. Market conditions are therefore favourable to employment growth. However, the new technologies will have the effect of reducing employment. For example, new harvesting machines developed in Scandinavia are capable of mechanising the entire process of felling, debranching and cross cutting; reducing labour input by a factor of 10. High cost considerations mean that only a few larger employers can afford them. Amongst these, further headcount reductions are projected to continue, as will employment of the unskilled and skilled operators. Those who remain will use the machines and engage in routine repair and maintenance. Finally, the shift away from the public sector, will also have a labour saving bias - albeit on a minor scale. This is because their private sector counterparts engage in multiple activities so that their employees either have a higher utilisation rate or get classified to other industries.

In **fishing,** the size of the UK fleet will continue to be restricted towards smaller vessels as fishing opportunities will be suited to short haul fleets operating out of Scottish and South West English ports. Access to fish stocks is expected to be fairly stable over the next four years, partly as a result of the EEC fisheries policy, although the future availability of certain basic species such as cod could decline, to the detriment of employment. The changing consumption habits and the move towards US-style fast foods are unlikely to improve market conditions.

In the light of these assumptions, the sectors' workforce is expected to decline across the board shedding 57,000 jobs over the period to the beginning of 1990; but with a much more pronounced rate in agriculture, owing to the new structural forces released by a changing policy regime (Table 4.5). The sensitivity of this forecast is +10,000, the most critical factor inducing the variability being the pattern and rate of change induced by the CAP.

Table 4.5   Agriculture, Forestry, Fishing Workforce: 1985-90

| | (thousands) | | Annual Percentage Change |
	1985	1990	
Total Workforce	655	598	-1.9

Source: IMS/OSG study

Summary

All three industries in this sector have experienced a decline in their workforce; agriculture markedly more than the other two. The decline in agriculture has been accompanied by increasing differentiation in the labour force - reskilling of some jobs and casualisation of others.

This is indicative of the growing 'industrialisation' of the sector; largely helped by the EEC's farm policy. Under it, agglomeration and innovation have received a renewed thrust to achieve economies of scale. Productivity has improved; the resulting growth in output has not involved increasing employment levels.

In future, however, the policy will be increasingly under strain because of mounting over-production. There are expectations that its reform will intensify pressures on farm incomes that have already halved in the last ten years due to mounting energy and chemical costs associated with intensive farming. The downward trend in employment will, as a result, accelerate - from an annual decline of one per cent in the last ten years to nearly two per cent per annum for the rest of this decade. From a total workforce of 655,000 there will be a reduction of 57,000 jobs by the beginning of 1990. The trend towards casual and part-time workers will intensify as will the trend towards higher skill levels among the permanent workforce.

5 Energy and Water Supply

Background

Given the multiple forms of energy in use in the UK, this sector covers four varied, but related activities: extraction, production, processing and distribution of energy and water supply. These are carried out on a large scale with a high degree of capital intensity, mainly by the oil majors and nationalised industries who dominate the sector.

The former are engaged in the extraction and processing of oil from the UK Continental Shelf. The latter, on the other hand, are engaged in single-product activities. However, this demarcation is not rigid. For example, with its Morecambe Bay gas fields coming on-stream, the British Gas Corporation are now also engaged in extraction and processing. But, in employment terms, such overlap is negligible.

Background information from trade bodies and secondary sources shows that total employment in the sector was 596,000 in 1985 (Table 5.1). In terms of size, coal, electricity and gas are the largest employers, accounting for over 75 per cent of the sector's employment. That said, it is worth recognising that the sector also includes a number of small employers. In both extraction and processing of mineral oil, a number of them providing specialised services related to oil exploration and refining.

Table 5.1   Employment in Energy and Water Supply Sector: 1985

SIC Activity:	Employment in 1985 (thousands)	Share (percentage)
Privately Controlled Industries		
13 Extraction of Mineral Oil, Natural Gas	33	6
14 Mineral Oil Processing and Others	22	4
Nationalised Industries		
11 Coal Extraction and Solid Fuels	212	36
15 Nuclear Fuel Production	16	3
16 Electricity	151	25
16 Gas	93	16
17 Water	64	11
Other	5	1
Total	596	100

Source: Employment Gazette, December 1985

The sector's national share of employment is, however, low compared to output (Table 3.1) reflecting the capital intensity of the operations. Furthermore, high though they are, the shares in national exports and imports (Appendices B.1 and B.2) do not show an important feature of the sector: its contribution to national self-sufficiency in all forms of energy.

Finally, comparisons of employment levels in either the peak years or the trough years since the beginning of the last decade show that the underlying trend has been markedly downwards. A notable feature is that the brunt of the decline has been borne by coal (Table 5.2). The only industry experiencing employment growth is extraction of oil and gas, due to the development of the resources in the North Sea.

Table 5.2   Energy and Water Supply: Evolution of Employment
             and Output 1971-85

SIC Class:	Main Cyclical Years:						Annual Percentage Change: 1979-85
	1971 (Trough)	1973 (Peak)	1975 (Trough)	1979 (Peak)	1981 (Trough)	1985 (Latest Peak)	
Employment (thousands)							
11 Coal Extraction and Solid Fuels	400	368	356	299	285	212	-7
13 Extraction of Oil and Gas	na	na	na	20	25	33	11
14 Mineral Oil Processing	na	na	na	30	30	22	-4
15 Nuclear Fuel	na	na	na	18	16	16	-3
16 Electricity	)						
16 Gas	) 388	353	360	279	273	244	-2
17 Water	)			60	66	64	-2
Total*	788	721	716	712	699	596	-3
Output (1980 = 100)							
11 Coal Extraction and Solid Fuels	na	112	109	97	98	67	-5
13 Extraction of Oil and Gas	na	2	na	99	110	150	8
14 Mineral Oil Processing	na	127	104	114	93	99	-2
15 Nuclear Fuel	na	na	na	na	na	na	
16 Electricity	) na	85	87	102	99	105	1
16 Gas	)						
17 Water	na	95	96	103	98	104	0

* Includes undefined activities as well

na: Not available

Source: Employment Gazette, Historical Supplement No 1, April 1985; and the CSO

Employment Trends and Their Causes to 1985

The postal survey included responses from 40 companies in oil-related activities including a number of small firms providing specialist services to oil companies. Their larger counterparts - in both the oil and the nationalised sector - are covered in the 22 case studies included in the study. This chapter provides an overview of the main trends in the sector.

Analysis of the survey and case study results identified the two oil price shocks of the last decade as the single most important influence on the sector's employment in recent years. Their effects have been direct as well as indirect; and traumatic in their totality.

The **direct** effect has been more visible in oil extraction and refining. On the negative side, there has been a fall in demand of about nine per cent between 1974 and 1985 (according to the 1985 **Digest of UK Energy Statistics**). This has been partly due to the price effect and partly due to the efficiency effect; the latter resulting from simple conservation measures as well as technological changes leading to fuel-saving engines in vehicles and industrial machinery. The scale of the fall created a large margin of under-utilised capacity in refineries built in the late sixties on the assumption that oil consumption would increase at three per cent per annum in the seventies and eighties. Closures became inevitable. In some of the case study firms, refinery capacity was either totally divested or reduced by up to 50 per cent. But this is a partial picture. On the positive side, the price explosion made it possible to develop the hydrocarbon resources in the Northern and Central North Sea, to the extent that self-sufficiency in oil and gas has been ensured till the middle of the next decade. New jobs have been created in the process. However, given the capital intensity of the offshore structures, their scale has been modest and their main beneficiaries have been the building and fabrication contractors rather than the oil companies. In terms of employment, however, the overall direct effect has been beneficial.

It is, however, insignificant compared to the **indirect** effect that has proved highly adverse to employment. The price increases caused two severe recessions which wrought an unprecedented decline in the demand of chief energy-consuming industries such as steel, chemicals, food, bricks, pottery and glass. This in turn has adversely affected the demand for oil, coal, electricity, gas and water (see lower panel in Table 5.2). The contraction in their employment has come through one or more of four causes.

The first and most important of these is the reduction and **restructuring of capacity.** Nowhere is this more vividly exemplified than in the case of coal mining. The NCB's **Plan For Coal,** issued in 1974, at the very least envisaged the coal demand to be maintained at around the 1973 level of 133 million tonnes by 1985. However, the out-turn fell short by over 20 per cent. Closures have become inevitable. Yet the programme of new investment in 'super mines' has continued where the use of new technology has meant that their productivity is markedly higher. For example, at Selby a workforce of 4,000 can produce the same tonnage of coal as 30,000 at less productive pits. Such restructuring of capacity has occurred across the whole sector in varying degrees.

The second cause has been **corporate reorganisation.** The capital intensity of the basic operations in the sector had ensured that, over time, employment had tended to concentrate in support activities across the whole sector. In this decade, employers have carried out extensive overhead valuation analyses with invariably a two-fold outcome: elimination of at least one tier in the organisational structures often involving major contractions in head office staffs, and a pruning of support functions, accompanied in some cases by renewed emphasis on sub-contracting. One major oil company achieved 20 per cent reduction in its overall headcount through this route. A nationalised industry achieved six per cent. In absolute terms, the numbers were quite sizeable in both cases. As Table 5.3b shows, since 1983 such improvements in organisational structures have been accompanied by improvements in quality of management (70 per cent) and in quality of physical structures (67 per cent).

The third cause has been the **new technologies.** Many of the companies in this sector are now major developers of different technologies as a way of automating the methods of production. They are also applying information technology extensively in office functions and it has proved instrumental in achieving corporate reorganisation. As Table 5.3a shows, around 45 per cent of the respondents in the oil sector alone had adopted new technologies on a considerable scale in 1985 in office functions. In mainstream production and distribution, too, it has been applied in process control instrumentation, enabling multi-machine manning and remote operational control; both of which have increased operative productivity. Mechanical technologies have also been upgraded. For example, new pumps have improved energy flow speeds and bigger road tankers have reduced the distribution costs and employment levels.

Table 5.3   Oil Industry: New Technologies, Working Methods,
and Business Aspects Past and Future

(percentages)

Column 1*   Column 2*

	Adoption in 1985			Future Adoption 1985-1990		
	Considerable	Limited	Negligible	Large Extent	Limited Extent	Negligible
(a) Areas of Technological Applications:						
Office Functions	45	43	12	45	50	5
Production Processes	40	38	22	33	49	18
Components and Materials	28	39	33	24	38	38
Storage, Packaging and Distribution	14	47	39	22	45	33

	Changes 1983 to 1985			Changes 1985 to 1990		
	Has Improved	Unchanged	Has Worsened	Will Improve	Remain Static	Will Worsen
(b) Aspects of Working Methods:						
State of Restrictive Practices	30	67	3	24	73	3
Amount of Surplus Manning	49	51	-	43	57	-
Quality of Management	70	30	-	70	28	2
Organisational Structure	77	23	-	58	42	-
Quality of Equipment and Premises	67	30	3	70	28	2

	Changes 1983 to 1985			Changes 1985 to 1990		
	Has Increased	Unchanged	Has Decreased	Will Increase	Remain Static	Will Decrease
(c) Business Aspects:						
Turnover (net of inflation)	64	21	15	63	27	10
Share of Exports in Turnover	26	52	22	37	52	11
Share of Subcontracted Business in Turnover	33	63	4	29	64	7
Product/Service Range	53	42	5	37	55	8
Number of Customers	53	37	10	51	41	8
Productive Capacity	54	41	5	54	38	8

Source: IMS/OSG Survey (Questions 2, 3 and 4)

*   Column 1 shows the extent of adoption in organisations in 1985/or change since 1983
     Column 2 shows the expected change in organisations over the period 1985 to 1990

**   Figures apply mainly to oil and gas extraction and processing.

Last, but not least, **job demarcations** within and between occupations have weakened and surplus manning reduced. For example, in the oil sector, 49 per cent of the respondents have reduced their surplus manning levels and 30 per cent their restrictive practices, since 1983 (see Table 5.3a). In particular, the share of un-skilled and semi-skilled operatives has fallen considerably while craft jobs are being structurally expanded to cover varied activities, as is shown in Chapter 16.

The collective impact of these four causes points to a three fold change: reduction in employment, higher labour utilisation and increased skill content of work. The individual effects of the four causes are not easy to quantify partly because they all emanate from oil price increases and partly because they are inter-related. The most dominant force has, however, been the reduction and restructuring of capacity.

Employment Trends and Their Causes 1985-90

Over the rest of the decade, the factors identified in the last section - capacity reduction, corporate reorganisation, new technologies and improving job demarcations - are expected to continue. If anything, the employers covered by our case studies expected the capacity restructuring to intensify. Not only will it cover coal mining, but also electricity, gas and water. For example, fifty power generation stations have already been decommissioned so far this decade at a time when five Advanced Gas Cooled Reactor (AGR) Stations are being commissioned. The latter are larger and technically more efficient. Also the cross-channel electricity line, now under construction, capable of carrying low-priced nuclear-produced French electricity, will come on stream. There are, however, about 63 per cent of the employers who expect to increase their turnover (Table 5.3c). They are mainly engaged in providing specialist exploration, repair and maintenance services to the North Sea operators. The scale of such services is likely to increase as the current generation of off-shore structures ages.

There are three other developments that will have a bearing on employment. The first is the recent major drop in the world **price of oil**. From the point of view of the energy sector's employment, its effects will be decidedly adverse. It will conspire to make coal and gas more uncompetitive and intensify the restructuring process. It will also undermine the pace of exploration and development in the North Sea: beyond the seven developments now in progress, no new projects are anticipated before 1990. Employment in the North Sea-based activities is expected, however, to continue at a lower rate of growth than compared to the last five years. Finally, reduction in oil prices is not expected to revive demand in the energy-intensive industries because all of them have shed capacity and therefore cannot return to the pre-recessionary energy consumption levels. In fact, as we shall see in Chapter 15, the structure of the economy has changed distinctly - and continue to do so - towards the low energy-intensive service industries.

The second development relates to the proposed **privatisation** of gas and water. Although the enabling legislation has yet to materialise, the pressures to improve the balance sheets are already there, and are affecting all aspects of costs, particularly those relating to employment.

Finally, the applications of **fuel efficient technologies** will continue in the rest of the economy. Their effect on energy consumption is best illustrated by estimates emerging from the case studies. These show that, prior to 1973, a one per cent growth in GDP required a one per cent increase in energy consumption. Since then, conservation measures and fuel efficient technologies have reduced the growth in energy requirement to 0.4 per cent for every one per cent growth in GDP. The GDP-energy ratio is expected to increase further over the rest of this decade. The implication is that the resumption of sustained economic growth in the aftermath of recent oil price collapse will not stimulate demand for energy on anything like the scale experienced before 1973. There are possibilities for diversification. For example, technologies are available for alternative coal use, such as synthetic natural gas, chemical feedstock or liquefaction. But against the background of world wide excess supply of energy, none of them are expected to be commercially viable in this decade. On the other hand, as Tables 5.3a and 5.3b show, over the rest of this decade the use of technologies in offices and other areas will continue to grow and the trend towards more efficient working conditions will also continue. Although their collective impact may not be as big as that associated with some of the factors discussed above, they will continue to depress employment levels.

Based on the assumptions outlined in the preceding section, the survey and case studies between them give estimates of the sector's employment evolution over the rest of this decade. The forecasts emerging from the postal survey cover firms principally engaged in the two oil activities: extraction and processing. It is clear that nearly half of them expect to reduce their headcount by the beginning of 1990. Significantly, they mainly cover larger employers (Table 5.4).

Table 5.4   Oil Industry's Employment Growth to 1990:
Distribution of Respondents

Cumulative Employment Growth Band (per cent):	Sample Distribution (per cent)	Dominant Employer-Type*
less than -10	16	Large
-9 to -5	5	Large
-4 to 0	27	All
1 to 5	5	Medium
6 to 10	8	Small
Over 10	39	Small

*   This indicates the types of employer dominating the result in the previous column. Based on their employment numbers, four employer-types have been designated for this purpose: **Large** (over 500); **Medium** (200-499); **Small** (under 200); **All** (no dominance by size)

Source: IMS/OSG Survey (Question 5A)

When the employment projections from the individual organisations in the survey and the case studies are amalgamated, forecasts for the whole sector are obtained (Table 5.5). In order to conceal the identity of the individual nationalised industries concerned, all component forecasts are aggregated. The sector's employment is expected to decline from 596,000 in 1985 leading to a reduction of about 70,000 jobs by 1990. Within this overall decline, in relative as well as absolute terms, most of the contraction will be borne by the nationalised part of the sector. The occupational changes associated with this forecast are given in Part C, along with the compositional changes.

Table 5.5   Energy and Water Supply Employment: 1985-90

	(thousands)		Annual Percentage Change
	1985	1990	
Total Employment	596	526	-2.6

Source: IMS/OSG Survey and Case Studies

49

It is equally important to report that the case studies emphasised that there is a good deal of uncertainty surrounding the future employment estimates of the nationalised industries. Much would depend upon the pace of the pit closure programme in coal mining, the timing of the commissioning of the AGR Stations, and the extent of electricity imports from France. An acceleration of these programmes could lead to an annual employment decline as high as four per cent. It was also clear that there was expected to be little prospect of slowing the rate of projected decline because of the need to restructure capacity and improve efficiency in order to survive the world wide energy glut.

Summary

This Chapter has analysed the evolution of employment - both past and prospective - in the energy and water supply sector. The principal conclusion emerging from the analysis is that this sector has been affected fundamentally by the quantum leaps in oil prices in 1973 and 1979. Together they have directly or indirectly contributed to a loss of over 100,000 jobs in their aftermath. They had beneficial as well as adverse effects on the sector's employment; beneficial, because they made it commercially viable to develop the hydrocarbon resources in the North Sea; adverse, because they created a marked drop in energy demand. The latter, in turn, has led to job losses through one or more of four related causes: restructuring of production capacity, corporate reorganisation, introduction of new technologies and greater flexibility in labour utilisation.

These trends will continue over the rest of this decade, abetted by the continuing applications of fuel efficient technologies and the shift towards low energy-intensive service industries in the economy. The recent fall in the price of oil in the face of world wide energy glut will, if anything, make matters worse because the competitiveness of coal and North-Sea oil will suffer, while any resultant economic expansion is not expected to be in energy intensive-activites. The sector's employment is expected to fall from 596,000 in 1985 by about 70,000 jobs by 1990. Outside the North Sea operations, the losses will be across the board, with the nationalised industries bearing the brunt of contraction.

6 Process Industries

Background

The process industries are essentially engaged in the conversion of primary inputs into intermediate inputs needed by a range of manufacturing industries. They are usually combined into two distinct groups. The first group covers iron and steel; cement, bricks and glass; and metaliferous ores and minerals. The second group covers organic and inorganic chemicals; pharmaceutical products; and man-made fibres.

Notwithstanding the obvious diversity in the nature of their products, these industries share two related attributes. Within each industry, product homogeneity is high compared to other manufacturing industries. Thus imports can constitute perfect substitutes. Furthermore, the homogeneity permits the use of mass (or flow) production methods, involving elaborate physical structures such as steel mills and chemical plants. As a result, the industries have high potential for economies of scale and the use of new technologies; both of which have employment implications.

Background information from trade bodies and secondary sources show that the process industries' share of national employment, at under four per cent, is about half the level of its share in national output, reflecting a high degree of capital intensity (Table 3.1). The relative product homogeneity, on the other hand, has ensured a significant involvement in foreign trade - in both directions (Appendix B.1 and B.2).

As for the underlying long term trend in employment, Table 6.1 shows that this has been downwards - irrespective of whether the comparison is made between peak or trough years - mildly till 1979 and sharply since then. In both groups the secular decline has been intensified by the recession of 1979-81. With the exception of chemicals, the secular decline is also mirrored in the output estimates. In 1985 the sector employed 779,000 people.

Table 6.1   Process Industries: Evolution of Employment and Output

SIC Class:	Main Cyclical Years:						Annual Percentage Change: 1979-85
	1971 (Trough)	1973 (Peak)	1975 (Trough)	1979 (Peak)	1981 (Trough)	1985 (Latest Peak)	
Employment (thousands)							
22-24 Metal Manufacturing etc	822	789	753	683	543	439	-6.0
25-26 Chemicals & Man-made Fibres	436	426	429	427	379	340	-3.4
Total	1,258	1,215	1,182	1,110	922	779	-5.0
Output (1980 = 100)							
22 Metal Extraction and Manufacturing	na	na	na	132	106	113	-2.4
23-24 Mineral Extraction and Manufacturing	na	na	na	111	89	94	-2.6
25 Chemical Industry	na	93	88	111	100	120	+1.4
26 Man-made Fibres	na	174	135	137	85	74	-7.7

Source: Employment Gazette, Historical Supplement No 1, April 1985; and the CSO

Employment Trends and Their Causes to 1985

The analysis henceforth is based on 234 survey responses and 63 case studies and provides an overview of the main trends in the sector. The employers in the sector identified three main factors affecting employment levels in the past. First and foremost have been the extent of **under-utilised capacity** and the need to reduce surplus manning. In the sixties, chemical capacity was expanded substantially on the assumptions that energy would remain cheap and economic growth would be sustained at the post-war historical rate of three per cent. On similar assumptions, man-made fibre production capacity was also expanded; and iron and steel followed suit in the early seventies. The oil price increases in 1973 and 1979 and the severe recessions that followed nullified the assumptions, to the extent that none of our case study companies had achieved full utilisation since the cyclical peak in 1973. If anything, the margin of under-utilisation had widened progressively; in some cases being as large as 50 per cent in 1985 at the time of the case studies. The two recessions are a major factor in this context because they depressed the demand from user industries, the extractive industries output being closely limited to that of the construction industry (Chapter 9). Superimposed on them have been two contractionary tendencies, rising import penetration affecting both this sector and its user industries (Appendix B.1) and resort to cheaper substitutes on the part of user industries. The outstanding example is the use of plastics in cars which has involved a shift in output between the steel and chemicals industries. The net result of these developments is under-utilised capacity; some of which is regarded by the companies as simply uneconomic, given the user industries' current cost and price structures.

The second causative factor has been the application of **new technologies**, particularly affecting employment in the production areas of the metal based companies. For example, under the modernisation programme initiated in the last decade, the steel plants have increasingly relied on the basic oxygen steelmaking process and continuous casting in marked preference to open-hearth furnaces. In one case study firm, in 1971 two per cent of output relied on the basic oxygen method. By 1985, this had risen to 50 per cent. The open-hearth furnace capacity was around 70 tonnes and production of a cast took several hours. Under the oxygen method, it can produce 300 tonnes in one hour. The sector has also witnessed a number of incremental innovations largely under pinned by information technology. Two areas where the employment implications have been obvious are process control instrumentation and offices. In the production area, they have facilitated multi-machine manning and job loading by weakening the divide between production and first level repair and maintenance. In a related way, in pharmaceuticals, microelectronics based monitoring of processes has significantly reduced the need for technicians. For example, in one case study company the re-equipping of a laboratory with the automatic monitoring of experiments led to a reduction in the number of support technicians from 60 to ten. In offices, new technologies have facilitated pruning or compression of hierarchial structures. For example, in one petro-chemical firm, the new office technology facilitated an organisational restructuring that involved a 20 per cent reduction in head office staff. As Table 6.2a shows, nearly 50 per cent of the survey respondents made considerable use of new technologies in offices and production processes.

The third factor, allied to the first two, relates to improvements in **working methods**. Since 1983 improvements have been evident in various aspects - especially in organisational structure and quality of management and equipment and the reduction in surplus manning. As Table 6.2b shows, more than two-thirds of the repondents had experienced improvements in these areas. The example of one metal manufacturer is by no means an isolated one. It closed two foundries and concentrated metal processing at a greenfield site adjoining its engineering works. Six business units were re-grouped into two, with all support and service activities integrated on a functional basis. This form of restructuring led to a 30 per cent reduction in the firm's headcount.

To summarise, therefore, the secular decline in the process industries' employment has multiple causes - some reflecting structural weakness in the face of recessionary pressures and foreign competition, the others reflecting the corporate response. Both sets of causes emanated from underutilised and uneconomic capacity.

Employment Trends and Their Causes 1985-90

Looking to the future, employers expected their employment levels to depend on the three factors cited above, overcapacity, new technology and improved working methods, because of their enduring nature as well as some new developments. First and foremost, the problem of **over-capacity** is expected to persist over the rest of this decade, for three reasons. First, the user industries in the UK are showing no signs of a major upturn (as shown in the following Chapters). Also, the rate of substitution of the sector's products for other inputs is unlikely to accelerate, except for the use of chemical products for engineering plastics. As a part of a long-term strategy, the OPEC countries are diversifying into chemicals and steel and are gradually creating a new marketing infrastructure in Europe. Foreign competition is thus expected to intensify. Finally, the recent fall in energy prices will ease cost pressures, but not significantly because of the historically high cost of energy and raw materials in the UK vis-a-vis our overseas competitors who will also be benefiting from lowering energy prices.

If the recent lower sterling exchange rates is maintained, this is expected to

Table 6.2   Process Industries: New Technologies, Working Methods,
and Business Aspects Past and Future

(percentages)

Column 1*   Column 2*

	Adoption in 1985			Future Adoption 1985-1990		
	Considerable	Limited	Negligible	Large Extent	Limited Extent	Negligible
(a) Areas of Technological Applications:						
Office Functions	50	43	7	50	44	6
Production Processes	48	40	12	50	44	6
Components and Materials	20	55	25	18	57	25
Storage, Packaging and Distribution	17	47	36	21	53	26

	Changes 1983 to 1985			Changes 1985 to 1990		
	Has Improved	Unchanged	Has Worsened	Will Improve	Remain Static	Will Worsen
(b) Aspects of Working Methods:						
State of Restrictive Practices	51	48	1	49	50	1
Amount of Surplus Manning	74	25	1	30	70	-
Quality of Management	67	32	1	79	21	-
Organisational Structure	69	30	1	65	35	-
Quality of Equipment and Premises	71	27	2	81	19	-

	Changes 1983 to 1985			Changes 1985 to 1990		
	Has Increased	Unchanged	Has Decreased	Will Increase	Remain Static	Will Decrease
(c) Business Aspects:						
Turnover (net of inflation)	68	18	14	78	17	5
Share of Exports in Turnover	51	34	15	57	35	8
Share of Subcontracted Business in Turnover	22	67	11	21	69	10
Product/Service Range	62	32	6	69	27	4
Number of Customers	56	32	12	66	23	11
Productive Capacity	56	35	9	62	31	7

Source: IMS/OSG Survey (Questions 2, 3 and 4)

* Column 1 shows the extent of adoption in organisations in 1985/or change since 1983
Column 2 shows the expected change in organisations over the period 1985 to 1990

help. In fact, expectations of increase in **turnover** are widespread - 78 per cent of the survey respondents expected an increase in part due to expanding product ranges and increased exports, although few of the interviewees were expecting the overall market to grow (Table 6.2c). However, the follow-up case studies showed that, given the level of spare capacity, these increases would not readily translate into employment. There were also some downside developments, especially relating to pharmaceuticals, whose output growth has averaged about five per cent per year since 1980. Here there was an expectation of a slowdown. This industry relies heavily on the NHS which, of late, has adopted a more restrictive stance through price reductions, restrictions on certain products and emphasis on cheap generic equivalents in preference to branded pharmaceuticals. However, indications are that the sector's overall output will grow at around two per cent per annum over the rest of this decade, with chemicals doing better than others.

Further productivity increases are expected to continue to reduce employment. The drive towards improved **working methods** is also expected to continue, and although the level of surplus manning is now much lower than in the past, many firms are still expecting to further reduce employment levels to become more cost effective. Over half the survey respondents expected reductions in restrictive practices, and improvements in the quality of management, equipment and organisational structures (Table 6.2c). The continued adoption of **new technologies** in offices and production processes is expected to further reduce employment levels.

Such cost consciousness apart, two other employment-constraining factors emerged from the case studies as being highly relevant over the next four years: **mergers and acquisitions;** and **investment abroad**.

The recent tendency to rely on debt-finance in corporate acquisitions has forced bidders to reduce all costs - including labour costs - in a short span of time. One taken-over case study firm in the bricks, pottery and glass industry had to shed 20 per cent of its employees in two years in order to meet the profit target set by the new owners. Under the new ownership, the emphasis was on profit rather than volume maximisation. As for overseas investment, this applies particularly to the multinational enterprises. For several of our major case study companies, expansion abroad was a more viable option because of the UK's high energy costs and low demand from user industries in the UK and financial incentives offered by foreign governments to set up production in overseas markets. Future expansion was therefore likely to favour overseas locations.

The assessment offered in the previous section points to a continuing decline in employment over the rest of this decade. The forecasts emerging from the postal survey (Table 6.3) show that 57 per cent of respondents expect a reduction in their employment and 43 per cent an increase. Their distribution by employer-size shows that the former group is dominated by large employers and the latter by small and medium ones. The finding has a dual significance: not only do a majority of employers expect contraction, but they are also the large employers.

Table 6.3 Process Industries' Employment Growth 1990:
Distribution of Respondents

Cumulative Employment Growth Band (per cent):	Sample Distribution (per cent)	Dominant Employer-Type*
-9 to -5	14	Large/Medium
-4 to 0	15	Large/Medium
1 to 5	8	Medium
6 to 10	8	Medium/Small
Over 10	27	Small/Medium

*   This indicates the types of employer dominating the result in the previous column. Based on their employment numbers, four employer-types have been designated for this purpose: **Large** (over 500); **Medium** (200-499); **Small** (under 200); **All** (no dominance by size)

Source: IMS/OSG Survey (Question 5A)

When the survey findings are combined with the more detailed estimates emerging from the case studies, they suggest an annual reduction of 1.5 per cent in the process industries' collective employment; a reduction of 51,000 jobs from a total of 779,000 in 1985 (Table 6.4) with a margin of ±15,000 on either side. The most critical factor is the rate of change in demand by the user industries. This decline in employment marks a deceleration compared to the earlier years of this decade: if anything, it is likely to be in line with the trend of the last decade. The forecasts have been aggregated across the constituent sectors to preserve anonymity of respondents but the broad trend is that, as in the past, the brunt of the decline would be borne by metal manufacturing and construction-related non-metallic mineral products. The resultant occupational changes are reviewed in Part C of this report along with the implications for part-time working, and women and young workers.

Table 6.4   Process Industries' Employment: 1985-90

SIC Class:	Employment (thousands) 1985	1990	Annual Percentage Change
22-24 Metal Manufacturing, Extraction etc	439	395	-2.2
25-26 Chemicals and Man-made Fibres	340	333	-0.4
Total Employment	779	728	-1.5

Source: IMS/OSG Survey and Case Studies

Summary

The process industries have experienced a secular decline in employment since 1971: mild until 1979, and intensified since then. In the face of contraction in home demand and rising import penetration, the decline has resulted in underutilised and less efficient capacity, and the adjustments forced as a consequence. The adjustments have involved the use of new technologies and improved working methods. Over the rest of this decade, the capacity problem is expected to continue; so will the adjustment process. Further corporate mergers, involving job reductions, are also expected. The lower cost of energy and the more buoyant outlook for user industries abroad are expected to favour overseas investment, to the detriment of UK employment. As a result, employment will continue to contract at around 1.5 per cent per annum, with employment falling from 779,000 in 1985 by 50,000 by the beginning of 1990. The losses will be concentrated in metal manufacturing and non-metallic mineral products. In a historical context, the rate of decline represents an easing compared to that since 1979.

7 Engineering and Related Industries

Background

The engineering and related industries are highly varied in their product mix, ranging from nuts and bolts, vehicles, shipbuilding , to high-tech electronics equipment. They include both capital and consumer products and combine techniques of mass production, assembly, batch and 'one-off' production.

Background information from trade bodies and secondary sources shows that the sector currently has a headcount of 2.5 million with mechanical, electrical and instrument engineering accounting for over 60 per cent (Table 7.1). In all, the sector accounts for over 10 per cent of national output and employment (Table 3.1), and features strongly in foreign trade in both directions (Appendix B.1 and B.2).

Since 1971, the underlying employment trend has been clearly downwards with a particularly sharp decline in the period 1979-81. This has been true for all sub-sectors. The long term trend is most pronounced in the case of transport equipment such as vehicles, ships, aircraft and railway rolling stock. Even electrical and instrument engineering - encompassing high-tech products such as computers and surgical tools - have suffered reductions (Table 7.1).

Significantly, although the employment decline has accompanied the output decline, the former's rate of decline is steeper, giving rise to improved labour productivity of around 2.5 per cent a year. Only one industry has shown a strong underlying growth in output - office machinery and data processing equipment, as the lower panel in Table 7.1 shows. But in employment terms it is comparatively small, with a headcount of around 75,000.

Table 7.1 Evolution of Employment and Output: Engineering and
Related Industries

SIC Class:	Main Cyclical Years:					1985 (Latest Peak)	Annual Percentage Change: 1979-85
	1971 (Trough)	1973 (Peak)	1975 (Trough)	1979 (Peak)	1981 (Trough)		
Employment (thousands)							
31 Metal Goods nes	576	562	532	516	414	381	-4.4
32 Mechanical Engineering	1,125	1,040	1,042	1,011	889	775	-3.9
33,34 37 Electrical & Instrument Engineering	1,018	1,000	964	946	857	832	-2.0
35 Motor Vehicles & Parts	503	509	456	433	355	281	-5.9
36 Other Transport Equipment	433	407	410	432	365	280	-5.9
Total	3,655	3,518	3,404	3,338	2,880	2,549	-3.9
Output (1980 = 100)							
31 Metal Goods nes	na	135	125	120	93	99	-2.9
32 Mechanical Engineering	na	115	120	109	88	92	-2.6
33 Office Machinery, DP Equipment	na	50	58	93	87	265	+30.8
34 Electrical Engineering	na	102	100	103	94	115	+1.9
35 Motor Vehicles & Parts	na	136	114	116	84	86	-4.3
36 Other Transport Equipment	na	102	99	93	104	93	0.0
37 Instrument Engineering	na	91	98	103	101	111	+1.3

Source: Employment Gazette, Historical Supplement No 1, April 1985;
and the CSO

Employment Trends and Their Causes to 1985

The analysis henceforth is based on 641 survey responses and 86 case studies
and provides an overview of the main trends affecting this diverse sector. The
survey respondents and interviewees identified four key factors that have
influenced employment in the past. The most important has been **the lack of
output growth** as the low rate of economic growth in the UK since 1973 hampered
domestic investment. For example, investment in vehicles, ships and aircraft
has fallen consistently since 1973; in plant and machinery it remained static
until 1979 and then had a step-increase and stabilised again (see Economic
Trends Annual Supplement, 1986). International competition has also

intensified, increasing import penetration and constraining the growth in exports. This has applied equally to the companies making mass-market items like cars and consumer electronics and to one-off items in heavy engineering. The more recent world over-capacity in sectors such as shipbuilding and vehicles has reinforced the market problems for the companies in these sectors. The only exception to this trend was in the office and electronics sectors where output has grown sharply due to market and export growth has been considerable, although again accompanied by rising import penetration (see Appendix B.1). Many case study companies saw their inability to compete in the past as being due to a vicious cycle of poor profits, inadequate investment and low productivity, particularly in the 'low technology' end of the sector. The problems were seen as deep-seated by the case study companies and yet to be eradicated by the removal of uneconomic capacity and general contraction since the beginning of the last recession.

The second factor relates to the improvements in **working methods** (Table 7.2b). Since 1983, improvements had been achieved in over two-thirds of the survey firms in the areas of surplus manning, where significant numbers of job losses were reported, improved organisational structure, and the quality of management, equipment and premises. Most conspicuously, manning levels have become a matter of top priority for a vast majority of employers in the sector. Layers of management had also been eliminated or streamlined in many of the case study firms. In a significant minority of cases, even replacement recruitment had become a matter of board decision: in several major companies there were targeted manpower reductions to be achieved annually.

A third causative factor has been the application of **new technologies,** in offices and shop floor alike, (Table 7.2a) particularly by the larger firms In the office area, 55 per cent of the survey respondents had adopted them on a considerable scale by 1985 in such activities as word processing, finance, stock control and wages; with the desk-top personal computer becoming commonplace. The most dramatic illustration was when one manager pointed to 2,000 square feet of empty floor space and observed 'That's where our clerical workers used to be'. In another firm, 2,000 employees were supported by five secretaries. The adoption of new technologies in the production process was less extensive, the principal areas affected being design, machining, assembly, and production control. Again, the large companies were the main users of the technology. In many companies extensive use is now made of Computer Aided Design (CAD) which not only increased flexibility and productivity greatly, but also helped to alleviate the skill shortages for

Table 7.2 Engineering and Related Industries: New Technologies, Working Methods,
and Business Aspects Past and Future

(percentages)

Column 1* Column 2*

(a) **Areas of Technological Applications:**	Adoption in 1985			Future Adoption 1985-1990		
	Considerable	Limited	Negligible	Large Extent	Limited Extent	Negligible
Office Functions	55	37	8	46	48	6
Production Processes	43	48	12	44	50	6
Components and Materials	27	51	22	26	54	20
Storage, Packaging and Distribution	13	44	43	15	51	34

(b) **Aspects of Working Methods:**	Changes 1983 to 1985			Changes 1985 to 1990		
	Has Improved	Unchanged	Has Worsened	Will Improve	Remain Static	Will Worsen
State of Restrictive Practices	44	56	-	46	53	1
Amount of Surplus Manning	67	31	2	36	61	3
Quality of Management	71	28	1	79	20	1
Organisational Structure	77	23	-	58	42	-
Quality of Equipment and Premises	65	31	4	76	22	2

(c) **Business Aspects:**	Changes 1983 to 1985			Changes 1985 to 1990		
	Has Increased	Unchanged	Has Decreased	Will Increase	Remain Static	Will Decrease
Turnover (net of inflation)	69	14	17	83	12	5
Share of Exports in Turnover	48	36	16	61	35	4
Share of Subcontracted Business in Turnover	35	50	15	32	55	15
Product/Service Range	64	28	8	67	29	4
Number of Customers	60	29	11	70	25	5
Productive Capacity	56	33	11	63	32	5

Source: IMS/OSG Survey (Questions 2, 3 and 4)

* Column 1 shows the extent of adoption in organisations in 1985/or change since 1983
  Column 2 shows the expected change in organisations over the period 1985 to 1990

design engineers. On the shop floor, Numerically Controlled (NC) and Computer Numerically Controlled (CNC) machine tools were becoming common place but the companies saw great potential for the further application of technology, particularly in respect of developing manufacturing systems and the linking of design, materials, and production activities. The user companies saw them as reducers of jobs in the short run and protectors in the long run - in other words, as a strategic response to the deep-rooted problem of uncompetitiveness.

The final factor has been the growing reliance on **subcontracting**, especially in this decade. This has been facilitated by the batch production nature of a large range of products in this sector. The survey shows that 35 per cent of the respondents had increased subcontracting since 1983 (Table 7.2c). This particularly applied to the larger employers. Subcontracting of services (as opposed to components) typically involved repair and maintenance, catering, cleaning, wholesaling, payroll, advertising, distribution or marketing. In manufacturing areas, the list also included the closure of machine shops and buying-in components previously produced in-house, although there were worries about a shortage of high quality competitive subcontractors in the UK. As a 'new' activity, subcontracting was viewed as a strategic change designed to achieve one or more of the following: economies of scale, albeit at one remove; ability to handle fluctuating demand; avoidance of skill shortages, particularly in the south; access to specialisms of both labour and up-to-date capital equipment; or the freedom to concentrate on what the respondents were good at - be that design, assembly, maintenance or consultancy - with some case study companies reducing their manufacturing and assembly activities to concentrate on sales and service as agents.

The redistribution also involves a permanent loss (albeit unquantifiable) of jobs as the contractors concerned are increasingly using the latest technologies and flexible working methods. As a result, subcontracting has a labour saving bias. Subcontracting has resulted in a redistribution of jobs both within the broad sector and into other sectors such as distribution, as was highlighted by the recipients of such subcontracting. For example, as is shown see in Chapter 10, as a consequence of the economy-wide redistribution of the wholesale activity, not just in engineering, the wholesale trades have gained an estimated 100,000 jobs.

One small countervailing factor particularly affecting the office and electronics sector has been the continuing inflow of investment from overseas either to expand operations already in the UK or to set up new 'green field' ventures. The overall number of jobs involved has, however, been small in relation to the size of the sector, amounting to well under one per cent of total employment in any one year. (See also Chapter 15).

Employment Trends and Their Causes 1985-90

Looking to the evolution of employment over the rest of the decade, the causative influences of the past will prevail, the major forces for change being long term; hence the emphasis in this chapter on the underlying causes prior to 1985 of lack of output growth, improving working methods, application of new technologies and subcontracting. Their relative importance will, however, change. Continued economic recovery at home and abroad - fuelled by the recent drop in the price of oil - is expected to stimulate the demand for investment and consumer goods and in the case of the former, notwithstanding the phased withdrawal of capital allowances under corporation tax. The extent to which the stimulus will feed into the domestic engineering and related industries will be a matter of competitiveness vis-a-vis imports in the UK, and in export markets. A competitive and stable exchange rate was seen to be important as the price elasticity of several of the sector's products was believed to be high. In this context, the companies saw the productivity gains of the recent years as, at best, arresting the deterioration, as overseas competitors, too, have been improving their productivity. On their own reckoning, some significant case study firms, in fact, have maintained no more than a status quo, despite impressive productivity gains. Import penetration is still seen as a potent threat to jobs, despite the fact that nearly 83 per cent of the survey respondents expected to increase their turnover. They expect to do this by widening their customer-base, introducing new products more closely related to market needs and expanding their exports (Table 7.2c). The electronics based companies, in particular, highlighted growing export opportunities as a major opportunity for business growth.

The case study interviews highlighted two other developments in relation to output. First, several major companies reported significant examples of the **closure of uneconomic capacity,** both in the past and planned, due to either mergers or intensification of cost pressures in the absence of new major projects - in, for example, the North Sea or the public sector - or due to continuing world overcapacity, as in vehicles and other transport. Second,

64

with the ending of the Government's commitment to maintain real growth in **defence spending,** a principal sources of stimulus to demand in the past is expected to weaken and affect electronic engineering and aerospace in particular, while telecommunications manufacturers are being affected by the liberalisation of UK purchasing policies. Notably, 1985 saw redundancies in these sectors alongside those in the more traditional engineering industries.

Continued growth in investment in new technologies is planned in both the office and production areas, nearly half the survey respondents expecting further large scale adoption of the technologies. Improved working methods have yet to reach their maximum potential, and the majority of respondents expected further significant improvements in the quality of the management and their organisation of work (Table 7.2b). A potential constraint on improving competitiveness reported by a number of the case study companies was, however, their expectation of continuing problems attracting and retain professional engineers and high quality managers who would be vital to the development of new products and new working methods. The sector was also seen by many to be focused on maximising profits and minimising labour inputs and was reluctant to increase direct employment in any circumstance. In a number of major companies, there was seen to be further surplus manning to be eliminated and there were planned annual manpower reduction targets still to be achieved, in one notable case of five per cent per annum. Finally, further subcontracting of both services and components is planned as firms continue to concentrate their activities where they see their competitive advantage lay. Again this is expected to be most prevalent among the larger firms.

The foregoing assessment point to a continuing decline in the sector's employment over the rest of this decade. Around 35 per cent of the survey respondents expect to reduce their employment. They are mainly the large and medium sized employers. Of the remaining 65 per cent who expect to increase their employment, the majority are small employers, in part benefiting from the continuing trend towards subcontracting (Table 7.2c).

Table 7.3   Engineering and Related Industries Employment Growth
to 1990: Distribution of Respondents

Cumulative Employment Growth Band (per cent):	Sample Distribution (per cent)	Dominant Employer-Type*
less than -10	20	Large/Medium
-9 to -5	5	Medium
-4 to 0	11	All
1 to 5	6	Medium
6 to 10	9	Small/Medium
Over 10	49	Small

*   This indicates the types of employer dominating the result in the previous
column. Based on their employment numbers, four employer-types have been
designated for this purpose: Large (over 500); Medium (200-499); Small
(under 200); All (no dominance by size)

Source: IMS/OSG Survey (Question 5A)

When these survey findings are combined with detailed quantitative assessments
emerging from the case studies, it is expected that the engineering and
related industries could lose another quarter of a million jobs by the
beginning of 1990 from a 1985 employment level of 2.55 million, with a
variability margin of $\pm$75,000 (Table 7.4). The implied annual contraction of
2.1 per cent is significantly less than that recorded over the period 1979-85,
except for one set of industries - electrical and instrument engineering where
the decline is expected just below the recent trend. The implications of these
changes for occupations and skills are considered in Part C of this report,
along with the expected changes in relation to part-time working, and the
employment of women and young people.

Table 7.4   Engineering and Related Industries' Employment: 1985-90

SIC Class:		(thousands)		Annual Percentage Change
		1985	1990	
31	Metal Goods	381	330	-3.0
32	Mechanical Engineering	775	710	-1.9
33, 34, 37	Electrical and Instrument Engineering	832	775	-1.5
35, 36	Motor Vehicles and Other Transport Equipment	561	490	-2.8
Total Employment		2,549	2,305	-2.1

Source: IMS/OSG Survey and Case Studies

Summary

This Chapter has analysed the employment trends - past and prospective - in the engineering and related industries. The past has seen one of a secular decline due to low economic growth at home and declining competitiveness leading to rising import penetration, constrained output growth, and hence reduced employment levels. The continuing introduction of new technologies, improved working methods and further sub contracting of work is expected to continue to impact on employment levels. The decline is expected to persist over the rest of this decade, albeit at a lower annual rate of 2.1 per cent. In the process, about 250,000 jobs are expected to be lost by the beginning of 1990 from an employment level of 2.55 million in 1985. The losses will occur across the whole sector.

8 Light Production Industries

Background

This sector is an amalgam of a heterogeneous set of industries producing either consumer goods, such as clothing, or natural resource-based intermediate goods such as timber, textiles and paper. Their production methods are also varied. Those like food and drink use mass (or flow) production; others, like footwear, rely on batch production. But, in most cases, the plant size is usually not as large as in other manufacturing industries. Nor has it been technologically sophisticated: most operations have been relatively simple and highly labour-intensive. Not surprisingly, therefore, the sector is exposed to strong competition; from the newly industrialising countries in the labour-intensive areas; and from advanced industrialised countries in the natural resource- or energy-intensive areas, like timber and paper.

Background information from trade bodies and secondary sources shows that in terms of its share of national output (Table 3.1) this sector is by far the largest of the three manufacturing sectors considered in this report. This is not surprising because of its inclusion of everyday 'essentials' like food, drink and tobacco which account for over 25 per cent of consumer expenditure. The abnormally high share of imports (Appendix B.1) is largely a reflection of the high labour or natural resource intensity of the sector's products and hence the relative advantage of overseas producers. In 1985, the sector had an employment level of just over two million. As Table 8.1 shows, the long term employment trend, irrespective of whether based on peak or trough years, has been firmly downwards; following the pattern identified in the previous two Chapters. The workforce declined by over 350,000 in the recession of 1979-81 alone; and another 250,000 since then. Output, too, has displayed secular decline until 1982, as the lower panel in Table 8.1 shows. A modest revival is evident since then, although it has a long way to go before returning to the

Table 8.1   Light Production Industries: Evolution of Employment and Output 1971-85

SIC Class:		1971 (Trough)	1973 (Peak)	1975 (Trough)	1979 (Peak)	1981 (Trough)	1985 (Latest Peak)	Annual Percentage Change: 1979-85
		Main Cyclical Years:						
Employment (thousands)								
41-42	Food, Drink, Tobacco	774	759	733	715	667	601	-2.7
43-45	Textiles, Leather, Footwear, Clothing	1,016	981	881	809	618	515	-6.1
47	Paper, Printing, Publishing	593	571	562	547	512	487	-1.8
46, 48-49	Other Manufacturing	614	647	603	595	502	439	-4.4
	Total	2,997	2,958	2,779	2,666	2,299	2,042	-3.9
Output (1980 = 100)								
41-42	Food, Drink, Tobacco	na	96	93	101	98	102	+0.2
43	Textiles	na	146	124	121	92	98	-3.2
44	Leather and Leather Goods	na	158	149	125	93	98	-3.6
45	Footwear and Clothing	na	106	104	111	93	104	-1.1
46	Timber and Wooden Furniture	na	138	116	117	90	93	-3.4
47	Paper, Printing, Publishing	na	109	95	108	95	98	-1.5
48	Rubber and Plastics	na	104	93	112	91	108	-0.6
49	Other Manufacturing	na	128	114	126	91	77	-6.5

Source: Employment Gazette, Historical Supplement No 1, April 1985; and the CSO

level of 1979. In the meantime, import penetration has continued to increase (Appendix B.1).

Employment Trends and Their Causes to 1985

The analysis which follows is based on 623 survey responses and 85 case studies and provides an overview of the main trends in this diverse sector. The survey respondents and interviewees identified the recessions of 1974-75 and 1979-81 and historically low output levels as being the main influences on employment change in the past. But there have also been a number of **industry-specific** influences which have had a depressing effect on employment over time.

In the case of **food, drink and tobacco** their domestic consumption has remained virtually static since the beginning of the last decade owing to four factors: the changing age structure towards the 'over 60s'; the strong trend towards health consciousness, 'eating out' or fresh foods; the 'excessive' revalorisation of tax on alcoholic drink and tobacco; and increasing retail power. The combination of these factors has reduced jobs on the shop floor. Increased concentration in retailing has also led to a marked reduction in the number of corporate customers and 'drop-shipments', thereby reducing jobs in the direct sales and distribution areas, as well.

In contrast, **textiles, leather, footwear and clothing** have witnessed a pronounced growth in domestic consumption, but mainly to the benefit of imports (Appendix B.1). Here batch production in small business units remains the norm, in contrast to mass production methods in the newly industrialising nations. Competition from them has proved difficult long after it began in the early sixties. Special tariff protection secured under the so-called Multi-Fibre Arrangement has proved a palliative - one that has moderated the pace of decline rather than its direction. Mergers and diversification have become an inevitable route to mass production and economies of scale - but with reduced employment. In one of the case study firms, this route has led to a reduction of 20 per cent of jobs in the last two years. The adjustment mechanism has also involved establishing operations abroad. In the last five years, two significant case study employers have started overseas production - one in the Far East to capitalise on lower unit wage costs and one in France to capitalise on design expertise. Both have also retained the contractual arrangement to supply the major UK-based retail chains from their overseas locations.

Paper, printing and publishing have also experienced a pronounced increase in import penetration from a very low base (Appendix B.1) under what is reported to be a triple handicap of high energy cost, overmanning and inability to modernise capacity in the face of falling demand from industrial customers at home. Its consumer-based products are part of discretionary spending which, too, has suffered from the recessions.

The same factors apply to **'other' manufacturing**, which here includes timber; furniture; rubber and plastics; sports goods and other sundry items. Underpinned by cheaper raw materials, better design and mass production methods, foreign competition has grown apace. In the case of rubber and plastics the problem has been compounded by depressed demand from user industries, especially vehicles and engineering.

Thus a combination of cyclical, structural and market factors has contributed directly to the decline in employment across the **sector**. Indirectly, these factors have intensified the drive towards more efficient production methods, involving the use of **new technologies** and **better working methods**.

For example, in food, drink and tobacco, computer-based systems have been applied to process control and office functions. There has also been a trend towards combining mechanical, hydraulic and electrical technologies to integrate production, packaging and distribution. In paper, printing and publishing, such systems too have been in evidence, especially in pre-press areas. In fact, nearly 50 per cent of the respondents in 1985 were making a 'considerable use' of new technologies in office functions and production processes across the whole sector (Table 8.2a). A related feature of this use was the improvement in working methods. Over two-thirds of the survey respondents had reduced surplus manning, and improved management quality, premises and organisational structure (Table 8.2b). These changes are best exemplified by a drinks manufacturer. A substantive upgrading of its plant led to a number of labour-saving changes: an automatic shift between different product lines with no downtime; integration of production, bottling and packaging; multi-machine manning with the aid of micro processor-based controls; first-line repair and maintenance work by operatives; and greater involvement of supervisors in production planning and training. These changes had directly reduced their employment by 15 per cent overall since 1982. In another example, an out-dated flour mill was closed, costing 150 jobs, the new mill is regarded by its owner as being generously manned with 18 people.

Table 8.2   Light Production Industries: New Technologies, Working Methods, and Business Aspects Past and Future

(percentages)

	Column 1* Adoption in 1985			Column 2* Future Adoption 1985-1990		
	Considerable	Limited	Negligible	Large Extent	Limited Extent	Negligible
(a) Areas of Technological Applications:						
Office Functions	52	39	9	44	50	6
Production Processes	47	39	14	49	43	8
Components and Materials	17	49	34	18	50	32
Storage, Packaging and Distribution	16	46	38	19	52	29

	Changes 1983 to 1985			Changes 1985 to 1990		
	Has Improved	Unchanged	Has Worsened	Will Improve	Remain Static	Will Worsen
(b) Aspects of Working Methods:						
State of Restrictive Practices	40	59	1	40	59	1
Amount of Surplus Manning	65	33	2	46	54	-
Quality of Management	66	32	2	78	22	-
Organisational Structure	67	31	2	66	34	-
Quality of Equipment and Premises	68	27	5	74	25	1

	Changes 1983 to 1985			Changes 1985 to 1990		
	Has Increased	Unchanged	Has Decreased	Will Increase	Remain Static	Will Decrease
(c) Business Aspects:						
Turnover (net of inflation)	75	11	14	86	12	2
Share of Exports in Turnover	46	42	12	49	48	3
Share of Subcontracted Business in Turnover	28	59	13	21	64	15
Product/Service Range	64	28	8	70	27	3
Number of Customers	56	28	16	71	21	8
Productive Capacity	65	26	9	71	26	3

Source: IMS/OSG Survey (Questions 2, 3 and 4)

*   Column 1 shows the extent of adoption in organisations in 1985/or change since 1983
Column 2 shows the expected change in organisations over the period 1985 to 1990

The light production industries have reduced their employment by nearly a million jobs since 1971 as a result of cyclical and secular forces, reinforced by organisational and market changes, increased concentration in retailing, and the introduction of new technologies and better working methods. In the period to 1990, although the same causative factors are likely to retain their influence, there is likely to be reversal in the role of one factor, economic growth. Its influence is likely to be beneficial across the sector save in food, where growth will favour up-market products rather than increased output and employment.

Over 80 per cent of the survey respondents expect to see an improvement in turnover, underpinned by an enhanced product range, customer base and production capacity (Table 8.2c). The prospect of a sustained economic recovery (now fuelled by oil price fall) has given rise to widespread optimism. To a certain extent, it is also a reflection of the feeling that 'things can't get any worse' after the unprecedented contraction in the recessionary period since 1979.

The problem of import penetration and the lack of international competitiveness is still a matter of concern to the respondants, who also see a need to replace uneconomic capacity. The technological applications and changes in working methods in the recent past are, however, expected to increase competitiveness and help reduce the pace of import penetration. Over the rest of this decade significant further applications of the new technologies are expected in office and production areas. The use of new technology is allowing the textile industry, for example, to become more responsive to the fashion market, by allowing more rapid adaptation of product designs and making short production runs more cost effective. In this way the UK's competitiveness is being improved relative to low-cost overseas producers (Table 8.2a). Changes in working methods are expected to have a less of an effect on employment levels in the future in some sectors because the labour reductions of the recent past have reduced the level of surplus manning and the scope for further reductions in manning. However, publishing, for example, still expects further significant reductions in surplus manning. Improvements in management and organisational areas are, however, expected to continue at a significant pace, affecting over two thirds of the survey respondents (Table 8.2b). The main thrust of the applications of new technologies and better working methods in the case study firms is on improving competitiveness by

73

enhancing their ability to produce up market consumer products for a fast growing UK and world market. In this context, the improved economic outlook is expected to generate funds for the improvement of productive capacity. The case studies showed, however, that investment in new capacity to combat the advance of import penetration and to mount an export offensive will be more than a matter of just obtaining the necessary finance. It will involve a change in corporate philosophy from managing decline and making profit out of it ,to one of 'managing growth and making a profit'. As if to underline the point, despite a number of takeovers to achieve the economies of scale, many respondents had not shown any organic growth in their employment since 1975.

Table 8.3   Light Production Industries' Employment Growth to 1990
            Distribution of Respondents

Cumulative Employment Growth Band (per cent):	Sample Distribution (per cent)	Dominant Employer-Type*
less than -10	23	Large
-9 to -5	8	Large/Medium
-4 to 0	17	Medium/Large
1 to 5	7	Medium
6 to 10	8	Medium/Small
Over 10	37	Small

*   This indicates the types of employer dominating the result in the previous column. Based on their employment numbers, four employer-types have been designated for this purpose: **Large** (over 500); **Medium** (200-499); **Small** (under 200); **All** (no dominance by size)

Source: IMS/OSG Survey (Question 5A)

The employers expect the long term decline in the sector's employment to continue for the reasons outlined above. But its pace will decelerate. The postal survey shows that 48 per cent of the respondents expect to reduce their headcount by 1990; and 52 per cent increase it. The former category is dominated by large and the latter by small employers (Table 8.3). When these findings are combined with the detailed quantitative assessments made by the case studies, it emerges that the light production industries' employment is expected to decline at an annual rate of 1.9 per cent with a reduction of 171,000 jobs from the 1985 level of 2.04 millions with a variability margin of ±40,000 (Table 8.4). In the historical context, the rate of decline is roughly half that recorded between the two recent cyclically comparable years, 1979 and 1985. The decline will occur in all industries; but with rather different rates in the component sectors The resultant trends in occupations and skills are considered in Part C of this report, along with the role of part-time working and employment prospects for women and young people.

Table 8.4   Light Production Industries' Employment: 1985-90

SIC Class:	(thousands)		Annual Percentage Change
	1985	1990	
41,42 Food, Drink and Tobacco	601	565	-1.3
43-45 Textile, etc	515	475	-1.7
47 Paper, Printing, Publishing	487	440	-2.1
46, 48-49 Other	439	391	-2.4
Total	2,042	1,871	-1.9

Source: IMS/OSG Survey and Case Studies

Summary

In the period 1971-85, the light production industries lost about a million jobs - more than half of them since the onset of the recession in 1979. The contributory factors were low economic growth; declining international competitiveness; changing market patterns; changes in the structure of retailing trades; and the introduction of new technologies and working methods. In the period to the beginning of 1990, the decline will continue but at a slower pace. Prospects of sustained economic growth will increase demand. Improvement in competitiveness - underpinned by new technologies and better working methods - are expected to help reduce the level of imports. Although less severe, the problem of uneconomic capacity is expected to persist in the absence of a major investment programme. Accordingly, employment is expected to decline at an average annual rate of 1.9 per cent - half the rate recorded in the period 1979-85 and involve a loss of another 171,000 jobs by 1990, from a total of 2.04 million in 1985.

9 Construction

Background

Like other capital goods industries, construction activity covering building, civil engineering and repair work is highly sensitive to economic cycles. Its customer base is broad, encompassing public authorities, firms and households. Changes in Government policy affect it directly through decisions on capital spending, particularly for the civil engineering sector and public housing, and indirectly through their effects on corporate and household behaviour.

Background information from trade bodies and secondary sources shows that the underlying trend in the industry's workforce, which totalled 1.4 million in 1985, is clearly downwards since 1971, (Table 9.1). However, within the workforce there are some off-setting changes: self-employment has been increasing and at the expense of direct employment which is declining, especially since 1979. In 1971, self-employment accounted for a quarter of the workforce. In 1985 it accounts for a third. The compositional change has occurred against the background of rising labour productivity. For example, the level of output was identical in 1975 and 1985; yet the workforce had contracted by over 175,000 over this period. In the national context the industry accounts for four per cent of employment; 20 per cent of self-employment; and seven per cent of output (Table 3.1). Given the nature of its activity, the industry's involvement in foreign trade is insignificant. Its performance is therefore highly dependent on a multitude of forces affecting the **domestic** user groups.

Workforce Trends and Their Causes to 1985

The analysis hereafter is based on 61 survey respondents and 30 case studies and provides an overview of the main trends in the industry. The respondents identified two related factors having a dominant influence on past employment

Table 9.1   Construction: Evolution of Employment, Output and
Gross Domestic Investment 1971-85

	Main Cyclical Years:						Annual Percentage Change: 1979-85
	1971 (Trough)	1973 (Peak)	1975 (Trough)	1979 (Peak)	1981 (Trough)	1985 (Latest Peak)	
Employment (thousands)	1,167	1,278	1,217	1,216	1,112	933	-3.9
Self-Employment (thousands)	342	439	362	343	388	469	+6.1
Total (thousands)	1,509	1,717	1,579	1,559	1,500	1,402	-1.7
Output (1980 = 100)	na	na	na	106	90	100	-1.3
Gross Domestic Investment (1980 = 100)							
Dwellings:							
Private	103	109	103	109	96	116	+1.1
Public	130	120	139	112	65	86	-3.9
Total	112	112	114	110	86	106	-0.6
Other New Building and Works	119	122	116	105	96	119	+2.2

Source: Employment Gazette, Historical Supplement No 1, April 1985; the CSO;
Economic Trends, Annual Supplements

trends: **domestic demand** and **sub-contracting**. The lower economic growth coming in the wake of oil price increases in 1973 and 1975 severely affected the domestic investment in civil engineering, dwellings and building works; the underlying trend since 1973 has been, at best, flat. Only new buildings and works have shown a sign of revival - much of it only in the last two years. The public dwellings component remains unusually depressed by historical standards (Table 9.1).

Against the background of depressed demand, the workforce has contracted, there being a close link between output and employment levels. However, productivity growth has shown a marked increase, especially since 1980; output having risen by ten per cent and the workforce fallen by over six per cent, breaking the long term relationship. This has come about through two routes: one minor and one major. Depressed demand intensified competition and many large construction firms moved downmarket to secure lower value work. Their relative size gave them an advantage through economies of scale and ensured a higher average productivity than that prevailing in their smaller competitors. The net effect was job losses amongst the latter and a step-increase in industry-wide productivity. But this effect is seen as less important than that coming from the second route involving intensification of division of labour and consequent specialisation. This has been achieved by contracting out work and buying in of non-direct labour. In employment terms, the latter has been more significant.

In the sixties, direct labour was distinctly preferred because the volume of business was growing. In the seventies, however, 'labour-only' subcontracting became preferable as a response to growing skill shortages and uncertain business outlook. This shift has intensified since the last recession. Uncertainty aside, it has proved an important vehicle for achieving high productivity in a competitive environment. As one senior executive put it, 'We don't think we can squeeze any more productivity out of our current subbies; the pips are beginning to squeak'. It goes a long way towards explaining the simultaneous increase in self-employment and labour productivity.

Thus subcontracting has been a strategic corporate response to subdued demand and the resulting competitive pressures. The response mechanism, however, had other elements as well - albeit subsidiary. These have involved some use of new technologies, mainly in office functions (where 52 per cent have been making a considerable use of it, Table 9.2a); and improved working methods through the easing of restrictive practices, reduction in overmanning and better management and organisational structures (Table 9.2b).

Reductions in overmanning has been facilitated by an increasing use of components such as roof sections and wall claddings prepared and produced off-site in suppliers' capital-intensive factories where bulk production has had a twofold effect: reduction in unit costs and increased value added. This is another aspect of subcontracting, but with one difference: it has involved **inter-sectoral** distribution of value added and employment, benefiting the process industries sector. Technological change has therefore had its main impact off-site and, apart from office areas, often outside the sector.

To summarise, therefore, the state of domestic demand has been the main influence on the evolution of the workforce in the construction industry. Its depressed level has forced changes that have involved greater use of subcontracting, of both labour and material and component inputs, giving rise to increasing self-employment and the application of better working methods. It is important to bear in mind that all these influences are highly inter-related.

Workforce Trends and Their Causes 1985-90

Looking to the future, the state of domestic demand will remain the principal factor determining the employment size. Exporting is not seen as a major growth activity (Table 9.2c) and is not regarded as employment-intensive. A clear majority of the survey respondents expect their turnover to increase (Table 9.2c). For many their expectations are underpinned by a number of what were deemed to be 'inevitable' factors such as tax reductions; easing of real interest rates; and involved increases in infrastructure renewal; repair, maintenance and improvement of the existing housing stock; and in home ownership. As a result, output was expected to increase at an average of between one and three per cent per annum, marking a departure from the trend of recent years. At the same time the trend towards subcontracting is expected to continue (Table 9.2c) as potential for higher labour productivity through subcontracting remains. It will most likely be realised as firms diversify. Of late, amongst larger employers there has been a clear tendency to establish divisions which bear less obvious affinity to conventional construction - for example, offshore structure, process plants and systems engineering - yet rely on a common core of construction 'know-how'. Currently, they are the fastest growing areas and reflect three key developments; an eagerness to move out of

Table 9.2   Construction: New Technologies, Working Methods,
and Business Aspects Past and Future

(percentages)

Column 1*   Column 2*

	Adoption in 1985			Future Adoption 1985-1990		
	Considerable	Limited	Negligible	Large Extent	Limited Extent	Negligible
(a) Areas of Technological Applications:						
Office Functions	52	38	10	43	47	10
Production Processes	15	38	47	17	43	40
Components and Materials	12	37	51	14	41	45
Storage, Packaging and Distribution	6	24	70	4	32	64

	Changes 1983 to 1985			Changes 1985 to 1990		
	Has Improved	Unchanged	Has Worsened	Will Improve	Remain Static	Will Worsen
(b) Aspects of Working Methods:						
State of Restrictive Practices	32	64	4	26	68	5
Amount of Surplus Manning	66	30	4	20	80	-
Quality of Management	71	29	-	77	21	2
Organisational Structure	68	32	-	70	28	2
Quality of Equipment and Premises	49	41	10	57	41	2

	Changes 1983 to 1985			Changes 1985 to 1990		
	Has Increased	Unchanged	Has Decreased	Will Increase	Remain Static	Will Decrease
(c) Business Aspects:						
Turnover (net of inflation)	67	12	21	66	21	13
Share of Exports in Turnover	32	57	11	23	73	3
Share of Subcontracted Business in Turnover	60	31	9	48	45	7
Product/Service Range	52	38	10	60	34	6
Number of Customers	60	23	17	76	19	5
Productive Capacity	59	20	21	59	37	4

Source: IMS/OSG Survey (Questions 2, 3 and 4)

*   Column 1 shows the extent of adoption in organisations in 1985/or change since
1983 Column 2 shows the expected change in organisations over the period 1985 to 1990

the conventional market as well as within it; an emphasis on engineering as well as construction skills; and a shift towards selling 'know how'. These developments favour subcontracting not only of labour, but of material inputs as well. Furthermore, they are weakening the traditional divide between design and construction, or between design and management, as the advantages of vertical integration become clear. A key factor affecting the development of such activities will be rate of improvements in the quality of management and organisational structures. Both were highlighted in the survey by three quarters of the respondents (Table 9.2b).

The foregoing assessment from the case studies suggests that the decline in the workforce is expected to continue but at a more modest pace than in the recent past. Expectations on the evolution of workforce forecasts to 1990 as emerging from the postal survey are summarised in Table 9.3. They show that 37 per cent of respondents expect a contraction and 63 per cent expect an increase. The latter group is, as in other sectors, dominated by small employers.

Table 9.3   Construction Employment Growth to 1990:
Distribution of Respondents

Cumulative Employment Growth Band (per cent):	Sample Distribution (per cent)	Dominant Employer-Type*
less than -10	13	All
-9 to -5	13	All
-4 to 0	11	All
1 to 5	9	All
6 to 10	2	Large
Over 10	52	Small

*   This indicates the types of employer dominating the result in the previous column. Based on their employment numbers, four employer-types have been designated for this purpose: Large (over 500); Medium (200-499); Small (under 200); All (no dominance by size)

Source: IMS/OSG Survey

When these figures are combined with those emerging from the case studies, they suggest a small reduction in workforce of around 0.8 per cent per annum implying a loss of around 50,000 jobs from the 1985 total of 1.4 million over the period to 1990 (Table 9.4). However, there was a considerable belief in this sector that extent macroeconomic policy would give a direct boost to the sector by 1990. If this boost does materialise, then the size of the workforce was expected remain. The sensitivity analysis suggests a range of 1.34 - 1.42 million, but under current policies the lower end of the scale is seen as most likely. Within either assessment, however, compositional changes in favour of self-employment are expected at the expense of direct employment. The implications of these changes for the occupational structure are considered in Part C of this report.

Table 9.4   Construction Workforce: 1985-90

	(thousands)		Annual Percentage Change
	1985	1990	
Employment	933	840	-2.2
Self-employment	467	510	+2.0
Total Workforce	1,400	1,350	-0.8

Source: IMS/OSG Survey and Case Studies

Summary

The analysis of the past trends has emphasized the cyclical nature of the construction industry and its depressed state of output since 1975. These features have not only led to job losses but also promoted, particularly since 1980, a restructuring towards self-employment as a route to higher productivity. Sub contracting has also been an important agent of change. Over the period to 1990, there is expected to be an increase in demand and output due to what are seen as a number of 'inevitable' developments in the macroeconomy, which will give a marked boost to output. Their precise effect is, however, uncertain. As a result, the downward trend in the workforce is expected to ease by 1990. The total workforce is expected to fall by 50,000 from the 1985 figure of 1.4 million under an assumption of current economic policy. It could however remain broadly stable at about 1.4 million under a more expansionary outlook. The trend towards self-employment, however, will continue as larger contractors restructure their work portfolio.

10 Distributive, Financial and Business Services

Background

Outwardly at least, the distributive, financial and business services industries display marked diversity in both the nature of services they provide and their user groups. At one extreme are specialised and customised business services, targeted at corporate customers. At the other is retailing which is highly standardised and consumer-oriented. In between, there is a varied collection of insurance, banking, law and accountancy services which are either specialised or standardised, depending upon whether the users are firms, households, Government or overseas clients.

Despite the diversity, however, these services share three attributes. First, with the exception of banking, all are amenable to self-employment because either the start-up costs are low or the value added is high. Second, they are intermediate services not wanted for their own sake (like leisure, for example) but for facilitating other economic decisions or transactions. Third, and most important, they are exposed to competitive diversification through new technologies or vertical integration. For example, some building societies are providing cost effective banking services through total automation of operations; while some insurance companies are exploiting long-established links to venture into corporate banking and estate agency. As a result, the inner boundaries of this sector are weakening, and the larger employers in it can no longer be readily identified with a single activity as defined by the 1980 Standard Industrial Classification.

Combining the activities in one sector, as has been done here, singles it out as the most important employer in the economy. Background information from trade bodies and secondary sources show that in 1985 it had a workforce in excess of six million, including one million self employed, which produced just over one fifth of the national output. It is also a major employer of part-time staff (Table 10.1). Outside the public sector it has also experienced the fastest increase in employment and self-employment. As such, it is at the vanguard of the so-called process of tertiarisation of the economy.

The evolution of employment, self-employment and output for the main cyclical years since the beginning of the last decade is shown in Table 10.1. However, two caveats are necessary. Both relate to the distributive services. The first is that the upward trend in employment in retail distribution as shown by the Department of Employment (DE) estimates is contradicted by alternative estimates produced by the Business Statistics Office (BSO) (See Appendix B.3). Analysis of estimates emerging from the survey and case studies support the BSO estimates and suggest that the long-term underlying trend in retailing employment is more likely to be down than up.

The second caveat relates to wholesale distribution. As an economic activity, it is neither satisfactorily defined nor properly enumerated in the national accounts. In this respect, the survey and case studies prompt two observations. First, employment in wholesale distribution has been increasing since 1975 partly because it also covers employees engaged in diversifed activities. Second, its output data, as compiled by the CSO, underestimate the underlying growth because they appear to ignore diversification: non-wholesale activities of wholesalers get classified to other sectors. In other words, its employment as well as output has been growing since the middle of the last decade.

Together, these two caveats indicate different employment trends for the two components of distributive trades. In the rest of the sector - covering financial and business services - there is no doubt about either the employment or the output trends: both are up. To a certain extent, the output estimates are spurious because they are partly derived from employment, treated in this context as one of the indicators of business activity. But other activity indicators corroborate a marked increase.

So much for the employment trends in the individual industries. Taken as a whole, it is clear that the sector's employment and self-employment have increased by over 680,000 since 1979. As such, the sector has been the main creator of new jobs in the economy in recent years. As for its compositional elements, data are only available for the employment component of the workforce (see Table 10.2). Two points are noteworthy. First, in terms of

Table 10.1   Distributive, Financial and Business Services: Evolution of
Employment and Output 1971–85

| SIC Class: | Main Cyclical Years: | | | | | | Annual Percentage Change: 1979–85 |
	1971 (Trough)	1973 (Peak)	1975 (Trough)	1979 (Peak)	1981 (Trough)	1985 (Latest Peak)	
Employment (thousands)							
61-63 Wholesale Distribution	na	na	na	902	903	964	1.1
64-65 Retail Distribution	1,951	2,063	2,048	2,133	2,051	2,153	0.1
81-85 Financial & Business Services	1,318	1,422	1,468	1,638	1,714	1,932	3.0
Total	na	na	na	4,673	4,668	5,049	1.3
Self-Employment (thousands)							
61-65 Wholesale & Retail Distribution*	725	na	680	636	698	815	4.7
81-85 Financial & Business Services	148	na	157	145	188	240	10.9
Total	873	–	837	781	886	1,055	5.8
Output (1980 = 100)							
61-63 Wholesale Distribution	na	125	110	113	98	110	-0.4
64-65 Retail Distribution	na	na	na	106	99	114	1.3
81 Banking	53	73	78	93	105	129	6.5
82 Insurance	90	100	93	101	107	134	5.4
83 Business Services	na	70	76	96	104	147	8.9
84 Renting of Movables	na	na	na	100	95	122	3.7
85 Real Estate	na	85	91	98.	102	110	2.0

na: not available

*   Includes Catering and Repairs

Source: Employment Gazette, Historical Supplement No 1, April 1985; and the CSO; Social Trends, 1986 Edition; and IMS Estimates

industrial coverage, growth has been uneven: just under 50 per cent of new jobs have been created in business services alone. Second, over 70 per cent of new jobs have gone to females and 65 per cent to females working part-time.

Table 10.2   Distributive, Financial and Business Services:
Pattern of Job Creation Between 1979 and 1985

SIC Activity:	Growth in 1979-85 in:		
	(Thousands)		
	Total Employment	Female Employment	Part-time* Employment (Females)
61-63 Wholesale Distribution	67	23	34
64-65 Retail Distribution	20	44	115
81 Banking	85	62	33
82 Insurance	28	12	3
83 Business Services	177	119	58
84-85 Banking of Movables and Real Estate	4	17	7
Total	381	277	250

* Growth in part-time employment (females) can be higher than growth in female employment when full-time female employment falls.

Source: Employment Gazette, Historical Supplement No 1, April 1985; and March 1986.

Workforce Trends and Their Causes to 1985

The analysis hereafter, based on 796 respondents in the postal survey and 67 case studies, provides an overview of the main trends. The respondents identified a number of causal factors employment patterns since 1979. Five are particularly noteworthy: externalisation and subcontracting; structural changes; organic growth in business; new technology and working methods; and changing job status. Each is detailed enough to merit a sub-heading.

a. Externalisation and Subcontracting

In recent years, there has been an increasing trend in the economy towards companies **externalising** their hitherto in-house service functions through permanent divestment or **subcontracting** on a one-off basis. This was highlighted in several previous chapters. In this context, functions that are relevant are either specialised (as in the case of computing software) or capable of economies of scale if mass produced (as in the case of payroll and payment through bank transfers). Two industries in this sector have been the main beneficiaries of the externalisation process: wholesaling and business services.

The wholesale distribution industry has gained as the manufacturers have gradually phased out in-house wholesaling because of the high interest cost of stockholding. With it, the wholesalers are also inheriting associated business such as transport, export and import and brokering. The case studies showed examples of wholesalers who now provide a whole cycle of services associated with distribution and sale of goods. This goes a long way towards explaining the increase in employment in wholesale distribution.

For business services, if anything, externalisation has been even more pronounced and comprehensive, involving both inter and intra-sector redistribution of jobs. Two examples exemplify their employment impact. Prior to 1981, a nationwide firm of accountants had 85 per cent of its income arising from the traditional audit services. By 1985, this had reduced to 50 per cent; the rest coming from specialist consultancy services to large corporate and public sector clients. Its staff had increased by 30 per cent, with growth concentrated in areas providing expertise in corporate planning, investment appraisal and market research. The growth has implied a redistribution of jobs between sectors. The second example relates to an insurance broker. Insurance companies are now increasingly relying on intermediaries for the retail function. Since 1983 this firm had increased its sales staff by 30 per cent most of whom were ex-insurance employees. This involved redistribution of jobs between industries in the same sector, promoting self employment at the expense of direct employment.

The case studies suggest that there has been a redistribution of jobs from other sectors into this sector by as much as 300,000, including 100,000 into the wholesale sector, out of the workforce increase of 700,000 since 1979.

b.   Structural Change.

Alongside the growth in self-employment, there has been a marked trend towards
concentration. In each of the industries in the sector, larger employers are
increasing their market shares. For example, in retailing competitive
pressures have intensified as a result of lower income growth and falling
share of retail goods in total consumer expenditure in this decade (see
Economic Trends, Annual Supplement, 1986 Edition). This has led to the
creation of larger units - the so-called superstores - that generate economies
of scale and lower unit costs. By 1984, 370 superstores were in existence (see
Euro-Monitor from the Institute of Grocery Distribution). Their impact on
industry's employment has been negative because they have either forced
closures of uncompetitive retailers or involved restructuring. In Britain, the
average number of retail outlets has reduced from 450,000 in the last decade
to 375,000 in this decade, (see Business Monitor SDA 25). As for
restructuring, this is exemplified by one of the case study firms. Since 1980
it had opened over 20 superstores and closed 350 smaller stores. Net floor
space had increased by 20 per cent and headcount decreased by 10 per cent.

Another aspect of structural change has been corporate mergers and takeovers.
In recent years, they have been mainly debt-financed. The resulting cost
pressures have made employment reductions inevitable. Two mergers studied in
retail and wholesale distribution produced reductions of between eight and 12
per cent in the first two years. Two other mergers involving financial
institutions produced 15 per cent manpower savings. In none of the cases was
capacity reduced. The reductions came through the centralisation of all
service and support functions.

c.   Organic Growth in Business

Alongside externalisation and structural changes, the sector has also
experienced pockets of organic growth which have not immediately displaced
jobs elsewhere. This is most evident in insurance and finance, both of which
have experienced a notable growth in output since 1979 (Table 10.1). In
banking, the creation of new services such as credit cards, direct debit and
credit transfers has increased the volume of business (see CLCB's Abstract of
Banking Statistics, Volume 2, May 1985). In the building societies, increased
savings and home ownership have increased business volume, branch networks and
employment. Similarly in insurance, recent tax changes, high savings ratio and
new products for the emergent social groups - such as single parents and

self-employed - have produced a rate of business growth not achieved since the sixties.

This growth environment has a double significance for employment. Not only has it promoted employment amongst the established UK-owned institutions but it has also attracted foreign institutions to London. Their numbers have increased from 403 in 1980 to 463 in 1985, creating an additional 12,000 jobs, equivalent to 20 per cent of new jobs created in the banking industry (see The Banker, November 1985). A part of this increase has been in anticipation of the so-called 'Big Bang', scheduled for October 1986 when the securities market will be de-regulated. Yet the fact remains that the job build-up by foreign institutions has been occurring since 1975 against the background of a growing demand for financial services.

d.   New Technologies and Working Methods

From the capital expenditure estimates emerging from the case studies, the distributive, financial and business services collectively appear to be the largest spenders on information technology outside the public sector. This was corroborated by the suppliers of equipment. As Table 10.3a shows, 63 per cent of the respondents used new technologies in service functions and 24 per cent in distribution; in both cases on a 'considerable' scale. The former applied to all office functions, including 'front office' terminals in financial institutions. The latter applied to elaborate point of sale terminals at the check-out in wholesale and retail trades, as well as electro-mechanical equipment used in the distribution centres.

Where technology is being used, it was seen essentially as an instrument of business growth and better working methods. A number of aspects of the latter had witnessed improvements since 1983: for example, surplus manning was reduced by 53 per cent of the respondents and organisational structure improved by 64 per cent of the respondents (Table 10.3b). In fact, new technologies and improved methods were the principal vehicle for accommodating a rising volume of services. Over time, as business growth has occurred an increasing proportion of it has been accommodated through productivity improvements.

This assessment is based on the fact that in none of the case study firms had technology **directly displaced** existing jobs. Used as an instrument of growth, its impact had been indirect. First, as business volume has grown, so has the

Table 10.3 Distributive, Financial & Business Services: New Technologies, Working Methods, and Business Aspects Past and Future

(percentages)

	Column 1*			Column 2*		
	Adoption in 1985			**Future Adoption 1985-1990**		
	Considerable	Limited	Negligible	Large Extent	Limited Extent	Negligible
(a) Areas of Technological Applications:						
Office Functions	63	29	8	64	32	4
Production Processes	27	41	32	28	42	30
Components and Materials	17	36	47	13	45	42
Storage, Packaging and Distribution	24	39	37	23	46	31

	Changes 1983 to 1985			**Changes 1985 to 1990**		
	Has Improved	Unchanged	Has Worsened	Will Improve	Remain Static	Will Worsen
(b) Aspects of Working Methods:						
State of Restrictive Practices	23	75	2	23	75	2
Amount of Surplus Manning	52	46	2	42	58	-
Quality of Management	66	32	2	73	26	1
Organisational Structure	64	35	1	65	34	1
Quality of Equipment and Premises	72	26	2	73	26	1

	Changes 1983 to 1985			**Changes 1985 to 1990**		
	Has Increased	Unchanged	Has Decreased	Will Increase	Remain Static	Will Decrease
(c) Business Aspects:						
Turnover (net of inflation)	80	10	10	85	11	5
Share of Subcontracted Business in Turnover	26	64	10	23	66	11
Product/Service Range	64	31	5	65	33	2
Number of Customers	70	19	11	80	15	5
Number of outlets	32	54	13	40	55	5

Source: IMS/OSG Survey (Questions 2, 3 and 4)

* Column 1 shows the extent of adoption in organisations in 1985/or change since 1983
  Column 2 shows the expected change in organisations over the period 1985 to 1990

90

reliance on technology. In other words, the displacement has 'occurred' in the growth process. But growth and technology have been so inter-linked that it is doubtful whether one would have been possible without the other. Whatever the estimated displacement, it is a matter of conjecture and debate. Less controversial and more obvious has been the second kind of displacement, occurring at the non-user end. Technology has endowed a comparative advantage to its users to the extent that they have been able to increase their business volume at the expense of less innovative competitors. In the case studies, this form of displacement has been far more evident in retail distribution, building societies, insurance and brokering than in banking. On the whole, technology has caused inter- rather than intra-firm displacement.

e.   Changing Job Status

As mentioned earlier, growth in self-employment is a reflection of two key features of the sector's activities: low start-up cost in some activities or high value added in others. The case studies also uncovered another factor, namely a change in status, from employment to self-employment, for certain categories of employees. Two examples illustrate the point. In 1979, one oil company had 1,300 employees involved in the supervision and running of its network of filling stations - retailing petrol, oil and confectionery goods. Now it has only 90, who supervise the operations. About 700 of the rest have become self-employed. They lease the stations and in turn employ 300 former junior employees. This changeover has led to a loss of about 200 jobs and involved a status change for 700. A large insurance company similarly changed the status of employees to self employed, affecting 10 per cent of its workforce. In this case, there was some inter-industry redistribution as well, because some of them established brokering operations which come under business services. In the sector there were numerous examples of such so-called job creation which at best involved no more than a redistribution of jobs between or within industries through changing job status.

To summarise, a multitude of factors has caused change in the sector's employment between 1971 and 1985. Their differing nature reflects the diversity in circumstances facing the sector's industries as well as in their individual service portfolios.

The major factors leading to an expansion in employment have been externalisation and subcontracting by sectors and organic growth in business; while structural changes, new technologies, working methods and changing job status have all had a contractionary effect on employment.

Workforce Trends and Their Causes 1985-90

Looking to the future, the employers expect the causative factors of the past to persist, though their relative importance is likely to alter. Additionally, two new institutional factors were expected to emerge on the horizon: reform of the Wages Councils and de-regulation of trading hours, both of which are expected to cause a step increase in employment. The evidence on deregulation is included here despite the fact that the enabling legislation was withdrawn after the completion of the fieldwork.

Taking the past factors first, the case studies revealed strong and widespread expectations of continuing increase in the sector's **volume of business** over the rest of this decade: over 80 per cent of the respondents in the survey expected increases (Table 10.3c). This expectation is based on the assumption that real incomes will grow at an average of about two per cent per annum. A higher rate would, of course, be even more beneficial as it would ease pressures on small retailers and wholesalers, as well as encourage the demand for financial services.

Growth will be widely based. All industries in the sector anticipate a rate of expansion which, at worst, implies only a marginal slowdown compared to the period 1979-85. As for the sources of growth, here considerable inter-industry variability is expected, again following the past experience.

Externalisation and subcontracting will continue to benefit four industries: wholesaling (because of rationalisation of functions in manufacturing), and business services, renting of movables, and real estate (because of rationalisation in all industries). In contrast, growth in retailing, banking and insurance will be organic: in the first case due to increases in real incomes; and in the other two due to rising market penetration, helped in part by the imminent repeal of the Truck Acts, regulating the mode of payment of wages and salaries.

Compared to other sectors in this report, distributive, financial and business services show the greatest growth prospects. However, the employment implications are less so because of the sector's continuing and increasing reliance on **new technologies** and **more efficient work organisation** over the rest of this decade. For example, 53 per cent of the respondents expect to adopt new technologies on a 'considerable' scale in offices; 65 per cent expect to improve organisational structure; and 65 per cent expect to improve the quality of equipment and premises (Tables 10.3a and 10.3b).

Following the past pattern, new technologies will have a two fold effect. In the user firms, it will displace jobs as output grows: in other words, it will complement employment but at a reducing rate over time. In the non-user firms, it is expected to threaten jobs by putting such firms at a competitive disadvantage. In either case, business growth will have a labour saving bias. This will be accentuated by two evolving forms of work design: horizontal and vertical job loadings, both involving structural expansion of a job. The former involves bringing more unrelated tasks under one job; and the latter, related tasks. In a climate of growth, new technologies are enabling organisations to redesign jobs along either of these routes and contribute to a more efficient capital and labour utilisation.

Both technological applications and changing job designs are indicative of the two dominant tendencies occuring within the companies in the sector; standardisation and routinisation. These are pre-requisites for economies of scale and lower unit costs which have thus far underpinned externalistion in all except the most specialised activities.

As well as the continuation of the causative influences of the past, two new factors were expected to emerge on the horizon: the proposed reform of the Wages Councils and the de-regulation of the trading hours. In either case, the enabling legislation had yet to go through Parliament at the time of the study. What therefore follows is a tentative assessment based on the assumption that both measures would have been enacted in some form in 1986. Their impact was expected to be felt mainly in retail distribution.

Taking them in turn, the case studies showed that the proposed exemption of young employees from the statutory awards by **Wages Councils** will be beneficial in two respects. Such employees were deemed to have a productivity level well below the average for other employees. Higher productivity came with training and experience. However, only a minority of the case study firms were proud of their training record. The rest relied on 'learning by doing'. As a result, it took more than three years for young workers to achieve the adult productivity norm. The statutory pay rates were viewed as not taking adequate account of this differential.

Secondly, and more importantly, in the face of rising competition, retailers have attempted to minimise the payroll costs by taking on part-time employees. Even where pro-rata benefits were granted, such employees typically had a higher natural wastage rate and, under the prevailing qualification rules, did not qualify for pensions. Now, however, a change is becoming evident in the retailers' attitudes in response to the recognition that product specialisation or diversification require different kinds of skills that involve investment in training.

In this context, two clear tendencies were identified: increased recruitment of young employees and greater job security for part-time females. The underlying objective is to offer more **permanent employment** - irrespective of age or sex - so that the necessary skills can be developed.

Finally, going on to the **de-regulation** of trading hours, the case studies suggested that in the first year de-regulation would be likely to increase retailing employment by about 20,000 at present levels of spending - most of it in the non-food area. The restriction on working hours as envisaged in the planned enabling legislation is a contributory factor, although a minor one. The major one was expected to be precautionary. In order to retain their market share, a large number of retailers in all sectors expected to trade on Sundays initially, notwithstanding what they saw as its questionable economics. However, as the shape of the new weekday peak load becomes clear, the long run effect on employment will begin to materialise. It is likely to be broadly offsetting for the two main components of the retail trade: food and non-food.

Volume of spending on **food** is not expected to grow significantly over the next five years. Sunday trading is expected to rephase the timing of spending across seven days. As a result, there will be intra-firm redistribution of part-time staff from weekdays to weekends. Given that the full-time staff complement is influenced by average daily spending, rephasing may also claim some full-time jobs. Furthermore, some inter-firm redistribution of jobs - from small to large retailers - is also expected as the comparative advantage of small firms, hitherto based on trading during unsocial hours, will be eroded. This second form of redistribution, too, will result in net job losses because the larger retailers see themselves as having the potential for greater economies of scale in labour usage owing to their size and technological advantages. Over the period 1987-90, intra and inter-firm redistribution was estimated to lead to a reduction of about 30,000 jobs at the current volume of spending.

On the **non-food** side, the outcome is expected to be less clear cut because of the complexity of economic and social factors at work. On the whole, de-regulation is expected to increase discretionary spending by providing an opportunity for impulse buying backed by a more intensive use of credit and charge cards. Over the rest of this decade, therefore, de-regulation would be expected to generate another 40,000 jobs. But when the overall gains and losses are taken into account, there could be a small net gain of 30,000 jobs, (20,000 initially and 10,000 in 1987-90) equal to over one per cent of retail employment. Given the margin of errors involved, it could well be negligible.

The employment assessment above suggests that the sector's workforce will continue to expand over the rest of this decade but at a slower pace compared with the recent past. The postal survey showed that 35 per cent of the respondents expected their employment to decline and 65 per cent expected an increase (Table 10.4). More significantly perhaps, increases as well as decreases are likely to be confined to smaller and medium size employers. The responses of larger employers showed no clear pattern. On the whole, their employment was either likely to remain unchanged or increase through corporate mergers or takeovers.

Table 10.4   Distributive, Financial and Business Services: Employment Growth to 1990: Distribution of Respondents

Cumulative Employment Growth Band (per cent):	Sample Distribution (per cent)	Dominant Employer-Type*
less than -10	15	Small/Medium
-9 to -5	5	Small/Medium
-4 to 0	14	Small/Medium
1 to 5	7	Small/Medium
6 to 10	11	Small/Medium
Over 10	50	Small

*   This indicates the types of employer dominating the result in the previous column. Four employer-types have been designated for this purpose: **Large** (over 500); **Medium** (200-500); **Small** (under 200); **All** (no dominance by size)

Source: IMS/OSG Survey (Question 5A)

When these results are combined with the detailed quantitative assessment emerging from the case studies, it is expected that the sector's workforce will increase by up to 400,000 between 1985 and 1990, with a variability margin of $\pm 100,000$ (Table 10.5). Both elements of the workforce are likely to share this growth roughly equally. In relative terms, however, self-employment will grow faster. In terms of industrial breakdown, financial and business services will show a more pronounced growth.

Despite the differential pattern, across the whole sector the share of female, part-time and young employees in total employment is likely to increase. Up to 30 per cent of the increase will go to young male and female employees; and as much as 50 per cent to part-time employees. As always, these are only orders of magnitude. Whatever their precise levels, the substantive point they underline is that the new job opportunities are more likely to accrue to the new entrants to the labour market. The occupational changes associated with this forecast are given in Part C as well as the implications for part-time working and the employment of women and young people.

Summary

The workforce of distributive, financial and business services has expanded since 1971 and more notably since 1979, with the onset of the recession. Both components of workforce - direct employment and self-employment - have grown. Causative factors such as externalisation of service functions outside manufacturing, rising savings ratio, higher market penetration and emergence of new services have had a positive effect. Others, like structural changes, new technologies, better working methods and changing job status, have had a negative effect. Both sets of factors have involved inter- and intra-sectoral redistribution of jobs. Their net effect, however, has been positive: over 600,000 new jobs have been created since 1979. The main beneficiaries have been female, part-time and young employees. Under the technological impact two tendencies are emerging: services are becoming standardised and jobs are also being re-designed to improve productivity. Both tendencies favour those who are flexible and trainable. The influence of these causal factors will continue over the rest of this decade; especially that of technologies and working methods as employers increasingly rely on them to accommodate the growth in business volume. As such, productivity improvements will increasingly accommodate the prospective business expansion.

Table 10.5   Distributive, Financial and Business Services' Workforce: 1985-90

SIC Class:	1985			1990			(thousands)
	Employment	Self-Employment	Work Force	Employment	Self-Employment	Work Force	Annual Percentage Growth in Workforce
61-63 Wholesale Distribution	964	815*	3,932	1,020	910	4,080	0.8
64-65 Retail Distribution	2,153			2,150			
81-85 Financial & Business Services	1,932	240	2,172	2,090	315	2,405	2.4
Total	5,049	1,055*	6,104	5,260	1,225	6,485	1.4

Source: IMS/OSG Survey and Case Studies

Two additional factors - if they do occur - are expected to have an impact on employment: the proposed reform of the Wages Councils and de-regulation of trading hours. The former will favour the employment of young school leavers: the latter would generate a small number of new jobs through competitive Sunday opening and impulse buying.

As a result of all these factors, the sector's workforce will expand at an average annual rate of 1.6 per cent, generating a total of up to 400,000 new jobs by 1990 from a base of 6.1 million in 1985. Sectorally, financial and business services will be the main areas of growth. Compositionally, self-employment, female, part-time and young employees will be the main beneficiaries.

11 Transport and Communication

Background

The transport and communication sector caters for a range of services, with
one common feature: they are involved in the movement of persons, goods and
information. Beyond that, they display marked variability in their capital
intensity, market structure and customer base, all of which have manpower
implications.

At one extreme, the sector covers the telecommunications network with its
highly automated operations that are continuously undergoing technical
changes. At the other extreme stands the self-employed owner-driver in the
road transport industry. Similarly with market structure. National companies
compete for freight and passenger traffic with small firms. Road haulage
relies heavily on corporate customers, and passenger transport on households.
The relative dependency on these two groups varies across the sector, ensuring
that its business volume and employment are influenced by a wide variety of
factors, as shown below.

Background information from trade bodies and secondary sources shows that, in
1985, the total workforce of the sector was nearly 1.4 million, of which
self-employment accounted for 103,000 (see Table 11.1). Employment in
transport was twice as big as that in communications. The sector's share in
the national economy in terms of output and employment are similar, indicating
neither extreme labour nor capital intensity at the aggregate level (Table
3.1).

The data on the evolution of workforce and output given in Table 11.1 show
that the experiences of the sector's two groups - transport and communication
- have been different. They suggest three noteworthy points. First, output in
road, rail and sea transport has experienced a pronounced cyclical pattern

Table 11.1   Transport and Communication: Evolution of Employment and Output 1971-85

SIC Class:	Main Cyclical Years:						Annual Percentage Change: 1979-85
	1971 (Trough)	1973 (Peak)	1975 (Trough)	1979 (Peak)	1981 (Trough)	1985 (Latest Peak)	
Employment (thousands)							
Road, Rail & Sea Transport	1,092	1,047	1,038	1,039	974	847	-3.1
Communication	435	436	439	413	429	419	0.2
Total	1,527	1,483	1,477	1,452	1,403	1,266	-2.1
Self-Employment (thousands)	65	70	77	87	99	103	3.0
Output (1980 = 100)	83	93	92	101	99	123	4.8
Road, Rail & Sea Transport	90	100	98	104	98	106	0.3
Communication	70	82	83	97	102	123	4.5

Source: Employment Gazette, Historical Supplement No 1, April 1985;
Social Trends, 1986 Edition; and the CSO

around a seemingly mild upward trend. Employment, however, shows a clear downward trend, particularly over the last six years. Second, employment in communication had a near flat trend till the early part of this decade. Since then, it has started showing a decline. This is all the more significant against the background of strong and sustained growth in output. This has been achieved through a marked improvement in productivity.

Finally, as in other sectors, the underlying trend in self-employment has been upwards. In fact, it went up sharply in 1984 during the miners' strike; but has since returned to its historical pattern. An overwhelming majority of the self-employed operate in transport as distinct from communication because the latter is dominated by two national organisations - the Post Office and British Telecom.

Overall, the sector's employment shows a secular decline since 1971. Since the beginning of the last recession in 1979, 186,000 jobs have been shed through employment reduction, and under 16,000 created through self-employment; a net contraction of around 170,000.

Workforce Trends and Their Causes to 1985

The following analysis is based on 146 survey responses and 34 case studies and provides an overview of the main trends in this sector. The respondents identified a set of four factors that have shaped the past trend in the sector's workforce: economic growth; changing industrial structure; use of new technologies and better working methods; and cash limits. Their effect has been either generalised or industry-specific.

Taking them in turn, the cyclical pattern of **economic growth** has directly affected the demand for transport services from their two user groups: firms and households. However, underlying the cyclical pattern there has also been a marked slow-down in the rate of growth of output in the economy. Over time this has widened the margin of under-utilised capacity and intensified competitive pressures in the transport industries of the sector.

This has coincided with the second factor: changes in the **industrial structure** of the economy. The decline in the bulk-intensive industries like chemical, steel, engineering, and drink has left over-capacity among the organisations involved in inland transport. Alongside this there has been a long-term but continuous marked shift in the pattern of passenger transport, as rising car ownership and more recently the partial deregulation of, and growth in, air transport has directed passenger traffic away from rail and buses. In sea transport the UK's falling share in world trade, combined with the containerisation of cargo and diversion of energy source - from the Middle East to the North Sea - has more than halved the volume of goods hauled by the UK-based carriers since 1973. At the same time, the foreign carriers have increased their share. These changes have had a two fold effect: reduction and redistribution of jobs. The latter has occurred within the transport sector, for example helping travel agents and others providing support services to air travel. The redistribution has also occurred **indirectly** between sectors, benefiting the car manufacturers in response to the trend away from rail and bus travel.

Just as profound has been the closely related factors of **new technologies and better working methods.** As Tables 11.2a and 11.2b show, since 1983 half the respondents in the survey made a considerable use of technologies, particularly in their office functions, and rather more had reduced overmanning. Improvements had also been made in the organisational structures and quality of equipment utilised (60 per cent and 64 per cent of the respondents respectively). Under their combined effects, job losses have occurred amongst virtually every employee group. The case studies encountered numerous examples in every industry in the sector where labour saving changes had been implemented in recent years. The following list provides some illustrations.

Sector	Labour Saving Changes Implemented
Railways	One-man operations; flexible rostering; open stations; capital substitution; electrification; and corporate reorganisation.
Road Haulage and Passenger Transport	Bigger and multi-purpose vehciles; use of exchange units in preference to repair of defective parts; increased reliability and reduced maintenance intervals; improved load and route planning; expanding motorway and trunk road networks. These factors have also affected employment in road haulage in all the other sectors.
Sea Transport	Trend towards containerisation; reductions in job demarcations; and use of office technologies.

102

| Air Transport | Greater reliance on intermediaries; computerisation of accounts and reservations; improved loading and route planning. |
| Communication | Greater automation in telecommunication and in postal sorting. |

The fourth factor influencing the past trends has been the **cash limits** set for the state-owned corporations. They have indirectly contributed to the overall reduction in employment; indirectly, because the recessionary pressures and over-capacity were already claiming job losses. Cash limits severely curtailed the scope for financial latitude.

Under the combined impact of these four factors, the sector's employment has declined. The compensating growth in self-employment has been modest, partly because the capital cost of new-starts are high and partly because the ability to provide a package of allied services has been limited. Industries like wholesaling have been successful in this respect as they have been more able to provide an elaborate collection of services associated with storage, distribution and sale of goods.

To summarise, therefore, the transport and communication sector has seen a reduction of over 250,000 jobs since 1971, with a majority of them since the recession starting in 1979. While in part the causative factors have been cyclical structural changes, new technologies, working methods and national cash limits have also been important.

Workforce Trends and their Causes 1985-90

Over the rest of this decade, the same causative factors are likely to retain their influences, although the employers expect there to be a shift in their importance.

The shift will involve the continued introduction of new technologies and improved working methods (Tables 11.2a and 11.2b). However, unlike the recent past, their impact will be moderated by growth in business volume. The survey shows that 80 per cent of the respondents expect to increase their business volume (Table 11.2c). There is now an expectation of a revival in the demand

Table 11.2   Transport and Communication: New Technologies, Working Methods, and Business Aspects Past and Future

(percentages)

Column 1*   Column 2*

	Adoption in 1985			Future Adoption 1985-1990		
(a) **Areas of Technological Applications:**	Considerable	Limited	Negligible	Large Extent	Limited Extent	Negligible
Office Functions	50	42	7	49	45	6
Production Processes	11	38	51	14	44	42
Components and Materials	13	38	49	8	48	44
Storage, Packaging and Distribution	27	41	32	31	47	22

	Changes 1983 to 1985			Changes 1985 to 1990		
(b) **Aspects of Working Methods:**	Has Improved	Unchanged	Has Worsened	Will Improve	Remain Static	Will Worsen
State of Restrictive Practices	31	65	4	30	68	2
Amount of Surplus Manning	56	39	5	50	50	-
Quality of Management	60	38	2	71	27	2
Organisational Structure	60	34	4	61	38	1
Quality of Equipment and Premises	64	34	2	66	31	3

	Changes 1983 to 1985			Changes 1985 to 1990		
(c) **Business Aspects:**	Has Increased	Unchanged	Has Decreased	Will Increase	Remain Static	Will Decrease
Turnover (net of inflation)	73	14	13	80	11	9
Share of Exports in Turnover	41	46	13	29	57	14
Share of Subcontracted Business in Turnover	53	39	8	57	42	1
Product/Service Range	71	17	12	72	22	6
Number of Customers	33	52	132	38	57	5
Productive Capacity	56	35	9	62	31	7

Source: IMS/OSG Survey (Questions 2, 3 and 4)

* Column 1 shows the extent of adoption in organisations in 1985/or change since 1983
  Column 2 shows the expected change in organisations over the period 1985 to 1990

for transport services at around two per cent per annum - a rate higher than recorded in the previous periods of economic recovery. The rate could be even higher if the sector is more successful in capitalising on the worldwide growth in air transport and also in halting the long term decline in sea transport. Neither of these possibilities, however, were regarded as practical for the foreseeable future. Growth in output is also expected in communications.

Against the background of the economic revival, two employment dampening tendencies will persist, one applying to transport and one to communication. First, the structural changes identified in the last section will continue. The employers did not expect to see any significant revival in rail, sea and road passenger transport over the rest of this decade. Business growth will be concentrated in road haulage, air transport and other supporting services to transport. In each of these industries, the scope for productivity growth is, however, seen to exceed the potential for business growth. Second, in the last two years, competitive pressures have increased in the communications sector. Growth in electronic mail and courier services has led to a more intensive use of new technologies and improved customer services in postal business and competition is being introduced in telecommunications.

Table 11.3 Transport and Communications Employment Growth to 1990: Distribution of Respondents

Cumulative Employment Growth Band (per cent):	Sample Distribution (per cent)	Dominant Employer-Type*
less than -10	13	All
-9 to -5	2	Large/Small
-4 to 0	20	All
1 to 5	5	Medium
6 to 10	4	All
Over 10	56	Small

*   This indicates the types of employer dominating the result in the previous column. Based on their employment numbers, four employer-types have been designated for this purpose: **Large** (over 500); **Medium** (200-499); **Small** (under 200); **All** (no dominance by size)

Source: IMS/OSG Survey

The foregoing points to a continuing reduction in the sector's workforce over the rest of this decade. The forecasts emerging from the survey are given in Table 11.3. They show that over 35 per cent of the respondents expect a decline in their numbers and 65 per cent expect an increase. The declines are likely to prevail across all the employer-size groups. In contrast, the biggest increase will be confined to smaller employers. When the survey forecasts are combined with the detailed assessments emerging in the case studies, the resulting projections suggest a continuing decline in the sector's workforce at an annual average of 1.2 per cent. Over the period to 1990 this implies a fall from 1.37 million of 76,000 jobs by 1990 with a variability margin of $\pm$20,000 (Table 11.4). Within this total, self-employment is expected to continue to increase. The occupational changes associated with this forecast are given in Part C, along with the implications for part-time working and for the employment of women and young people.

Table 11.4   Transport and Communications Workforce: 1985-90

	(thousands)		Annual Percentage Change
	1985	1990	
Employment	1,266	1,180	-1.5
Self-Employment	103	113	+2.5
Total Workforce	1,369	1,293	-1.2

Source: IMS/OSG Survey and Case Studies

Summary

This Chapter has examined the past and future trends in the workforce of the transport and communication sector. Since 1971, the sector has lost over 250,000 jobs; nearly three quarters of them since the beginning of the last recession. The decline has been across the sector but most of it has been concentrated in the transport industries. There has been some growth in self-employment; but not enough to arrest the downward trend in direct employment. The decline has been caused by low economic growth, contraction in bulk-producing manufacturing industries, applications of new technologies and better working methods, and cash limits.

Over the rest of this decade, the causative factors will change somewhat. Business volume is expected to expand but will be narrowly based; benefiting mainly road haulage, air transport and other supporting activities as well as communications. The drive towards new technologies and better working methods under competitive and cost pressures will continue and restrain employment growth through higher productivity.

Accordingly, over the period to 1990, the decline in the sector's workforce will continue at an annual rate of 1.2 per cent, a rate slower than in the past. The upward trend in the share taken by self-employment will however be maintained. The total decline is expected to be of 75,000 jobs by 1990, from a total of 1.37 million in 1985.

12 Leisure and Related Services

Background

This sector covers all **marketed** services not included in the previous two Chapters. As is inevitable in such a residual category, the sector is particularly heterogeneous. The activities covered vary in their customer mix; for example, hotels and catering have a broad customer-base consisting of firms, households and tourists. Recreational services are largely directed at households. Others, like cleaning and research and development, are directed at firms. Their method of production is also varied; for example, hairdressing (classified under personal services) and catering involve production and distribution simultaneously. Those like recreation and cultural services have a large 'self-service' element. Some, like research and development, are knowledge-intensive; others, like hotels and repairs, are capital-intensive. Labour-intensity varies across the sector, being more pronounced in catering and personal services.

Background information from trade bodies and secondary sources shows the sector's importance in the national context. In 1985, it had a workforce of over 2.5 million people, accounting for 10 per cent of employment and over five per cent of self-employment in the economy (Table 3.1) Its contribution to output and foreign trade is difficult to assess. The data on many aspects of its activities are unusually unreliable because corporate death rates are high and small firms predominate. The latter are exempt from various Government sponsored statistical enquiries. The sector's activities are also highly exposed to the 'black economy' (e.g. car repairs; hairdressing).

Table 12.1 gives the estimates of employment and self-employment for the main cyclical years since the beginning of the last decade. It is clear that although the sector's workforce is subject to the cyclical influences there is a clear upward trend, with particularly pronounced increases since 1979 in self-employment.

In sectoral terms the patterns of recent growth can be clustered into three groups,

Growth Group: Hotels and catering; cleaning services; R&D.

Static Group: Recreational and cultural services; repair of goods.

Declining Group: Personal services.

Table 12.1   Leisure and Related Services: Evolution of Workforce 1971-85

SIC Class:	Main Cyclical Years:					1985 (Latest Peak)	Annual Percentage Change: 1979-85
	1971 (Trough)	1973 (Peak)	1975 (Trough)	1979 (Peak)	1981 (Trough)		
Employment (thousands)							
66 Hotel and Catering	691	795	830	938	937	1,041	1.8
97 Recreation and Cultural Services	na	na	389	422	424	426	0.2
67 Repairs of Goods and Vehicles	na	na	178	200	200	206	0.5
92 Cleaning Services	na	na	170	175	179	214	3.7
94 Research and Development	na	na	117	125	122	132	0.9
98 Personal Services	na	na	92	196	177	176	-1.7
Total	na	na	1,776	2,056	2,039	2,195	1.1
Self-Employment*	261	247	268	234	288	467	16.6
Total Workforce	na	na	2,044	2,290	2,327	2,662	2.7

* Excludes Hotels and Catering; and Repairs of Goods and Vehicles

na: Not available

Source: Employment Gazette, Historical Supplement No 1, April 1985; other unpublished Department of Employment estimates; Social Trends, 1986 Edition.

This variable pattern does not detract from the rising importance of the sector in the national context. After the distributive, financial and business services sector, it has been the main area of job creation since at least the middle of the last decade. Indeed, the pattern of job creation in these two sectors have two other points of commonality. First, in both of them, intra-sectoral variability is evident, with the fastest growth occurring in industries providing **business** services. Second, job creation has focused mainly on female and part-time employees. This is even more pronounced in the leisure and other services sector, as can be seen in Table 12.2.

Workforce Trends and Their Causes to 1985

The following analysis is based on 277 survey responses and 60 case studies and provides an overview of the main trends in the sector. It shows that economic expansion has been the driving force in the evolution of employment since 1971. It has given rise to a number of both industry-specific and generalised factors. These are considered in turn below, first under industry headings and then under a general heading.

a.   Hotels and Catering

This industry has been subject to cyclical pressures through changes in household discretionary income, corporate profits and the exchange rate. These in turn have affected the industry's employment level. However, the underlying trend in employment has been upwards since 1971 as a **net** result of three factors: with two having a positive influence and one a negative influence.

On the **positive** side, since the beginning of the last decade there has been a marked growth in overseas tourists coming to the UK - a trend reinforced by a growth in domestic tourism in this decade. Many of the main resorts have been substantially upgraded. More beneficial, however, has been the creation of new capacity. Under the emerging social trends, consumption of wine and lager is increasing at the expense of beer and spirits and this has led a number of our case study firms to invest heavily in upgrading their pubs to wine bars, catering for full meals and drinks service. The trend towards eating out has also called for a substantial investment in creating nationwide retail outlets and 'fast food' chains. The creation of this new capacity, in turn, has resulted from two sources: an increase in the number of single person households and growth in leisure activities on the back of rising affluence of those in work. The former has mitigated against the economies of scale in the

Table 12.2   Leisure and Other Services: Patterns of Employment Growth Between 1979 and 1985

SIC Activity:	Growth in 1979-85 in: (thousands)		
	Total Employment	Female Employment	Part-time (female) Employment
Leisure Services:			
66 Hotels and Catering	103	58	84
97 Recreation and Cultural Services	4	22	19
Sub Total	107	80	103
Other Services:			
67 Repairs of Goods and Vehicles	6	9	9
92 Cleaning Services	39	30*	35*
94 Research and Development	8	6	0
98 Personal Services	-20	-15	-7
Sub Total	33	30	37
Sectoral Total	140	110	140

* IMS Estimates

Source: Employment Gazette, Historical Supplement No 1, April 1985, and March 1986

consumption of food at home, and the latter has increased its 'time' cost.

On the **negative** side, there has been a trend towards leasing arrangements which have a distinct job saving bias. Since 1978, the lack of developable land in the inner city areas for new hotel construction led a number of major hoteliers to expand their business through a leasing arrangement. Under it, a hotel group offers a total management package to medium or small size hoteliers lacking expertise and/or inclination to expand their businesses. The owners are guaranteed a fixed return on capital in exchange for the day-to-day management of their hotels. In principle, such an arrangement cannot be expected to have significant employment implications, because they merely involve transfer of management functions. In practice, they have. The managing groups have sought to run such hotels as 'piggy-back' operations using head office facilities for marketing, buying, reservations, training, recruitment and payroll. For example, in 1982, one case study hotel group took over the management of a country resort with 60 bedrooms, a discotheque, a casino and a restaurant. Prior to take-over, the resort had 40 employees on full-time equivalent basis. Since then, the numbers have come down to 32, even though the turnover has increased by a third.

b.   Recreation and Cultural Services

These services have three components: entertainment (including radio, television and theatres, and film production); libraries, museums and art galleries; and sport and other recreational services. The case studies highlight the following trends since the middle of the last decade:

Entertainment	The trend has been up; except in the case of film production and distribution where employment has declined.
Libraries, museums and galleries	The trend was up in the last decade but has since reversed under the impact of public sector cash limits and reduced subsidies.
Sport and recreational services	Here, too, the trend was sharply up until 1981 and has since lessened because of reductions in public sector spending.

112

These activities have been affected by two social trends: internalisation of leisure within homes and increased health consciousness, (see relevant estimates in Social Trends, 1986 Edition).

Availability and ownership of new home-based entertainments products such as colour television, video recorders and games has gradually shifted the focus of entertainment from the market place to home. Entertainment has thus increasingly acquired a 'self service' element. This, in turn, has stimulated activities in the 'software' producing industries like television and radio broadcasting; but at the expense of, say, film production as the published estimates on cinema attendance corroborate.

As for sports activities, there has been a decline in the spectator sports; adversely affecting employment at places such as football grounds. But this has been compensated by an increase in participant sports which has helped employment in private and until recently public facilities.

Overall employment in this sector grew rapidly until 1979 but has since shown a more stable level as public spending has been cut back.

c.   Repair of Goods and Vehicles

Here, the employment trend has been affected by two offsetting factors. On the positive side, there has been a continuous increase in the ownership of vehicles and household goods since the beginning of the last decade. For example, the number of registered vehicles increased from about 17 million to 21 million over the decade to 1984.

In its wake, growth in ownership has created a rising need for the after-sales services and promoted employment. Over time, however, this has been increasingly affected by improved product reliability, less frequent servicing, a tendency to replace rather than repair defective parts and growth in the number of 'quick-fit' replacement centres; all made possible by continuous technical changes at the production end.

d.   Cleaning Services

Of all the industries in the sector, cleaning services has had the fastest growth in employment. In substantial measure, growth has occurred through a redistribution between sectors in that it has resulted from the growing trend

113

towards the subcontracting of the cleaning functions on the part of public and private sector employers. This represents a transfer of employment from one sector (e.g. manufacturing) to another (eg. services). In terms of headcount, however, externalisation and subcontracting have caused a net increase in jobs because the case studies have shown that contract cleaners tend to employ more part-time employees and have more flexible manning strategies. For example, one case study firm providing cleaning services to various health authorities had twice as many employees as the authorities had previously when cleaning was done in-house. However, 90 per cent of the firms staff were part-time, their annual growth since 1981 averaging 15 per cent. The remaining 10 per cent were managerial and sales employees, responsible for recruiting and administering the new business.

e.   Research and Development

Here, the growth in employment has been partly organic and partly diversionary. The organic component is a reflection of growing complexity of operations in every area of corporate life, raising their knowledge component. A number of the case study firms have relied on research establishments as a source of accumulated knowledge and specialism, in the face of falling average life of industrial and household products. Public bodies, too, are increasingly relying on outside specialists for research studies.

The diversionary element has originated from corporate restructuring. The case studies showed that a number of employers in this industry are subsidiaries of significant companies. To the extent that subsidiaries have been created and treated as independent profit centres, their activities are no longer classified as those applying to their parent companies. For example, a firm engaged in the production of metal containers decentralised all activities. This involved the formation of an R & D subsidiary which was subsequently relocated to one of the science parks. There it employed 60 scientists, engineers and technologists and over 100 technicians.

f.   Personal Services

In the main areas of this industry - hairdressing, and laundries and dry cleaning - traditional employment has declined. In the first case, it has been due to the growth of the black economy and self employment; and in the second due to rising ownership of washing machines and declining capacity as a result of increasing industrial concentration and competition.

Generalised Factors

So much for the industry-specific factors. Discussion of them now leads to some general observations about employment change in the sector.

As shown above, factors such as infrastructure creation, internalisation of leisure, and externalisation of business services all reflect the socio-economic changes that have been occurring at least since the beginning of the last decade.

The nature of the production methods is now changing. With large firms moving into the sector gradually, competitive presures are increasing, **new technologies** are beginning to be utilised and **working methods** becoming more efficient. Even hotels and catering, hitherto looked upon as the traditional service industry, is increasingly fragmenting and standardising the functions that permit the economies of scale through the use of new technologies.

In fact, the survey showed that 47 per cent of the respondents were making 'considerable' use of new technologies in office functions in 1985 (see Table 12.3a). In areas such as garage repairs, kitchen activities and contract cleaning, electro-mechanical technologies were also being used intensively amongst the larger employers. Apart from new technologies, the working methods are also changing. For example, since 1983 over half the sampled employers had recorded improvement in labour utilisation, through reductions in surplus manning; and improvements in management quality, organisational structure and capital equipment (see Table 12.3b). The implication of all these changes is that, like agriculture, service industries too are gradually becoming 'industrialised' and susceptible to improved productivity growth.

Table 12.3   Leisure and Other Services: New Technologies, Working Methods, and Business Aspects Past and Future

(percentages)

Column 1*   Column 2*

(a) **Areas of Technological Applications:**	Adoption in 1985			Future Adoption 1985–1990		
	Considerable	Limited	Negligible	Large Extent	Limited Extent	Negligible
Office Functions	47	38	15	48	39	13
Production Processes	18	46	36	16	54	30
Components and Materials	15	39	46	10	46	44
Storage, Packaging and Distribution	13	30	57	15	35	50

(b) **Aspects of Working Methods:**	Changes 1983 to 1985			Changes 1985 to 1990		
	Has Improved	Unchanged	Has Worsened	Will Improve	Remain Static	Will Worsen
State of Restrictive Practices	25	73	3	27	71	2
Amount of Surplus Manning	53	45	2	50	50	-
Quality of Management	64	34	2	69	31	-
Organisational Structure	64	35	1	62	38	-
Quality of Equipment and Premises	69	28	3	74	26	-

(c) **Business Aspects:**	Changes 1983 to 1985			Changes 1985 to 1990		
	Has Increased	Unchanged	Has Decreased	Will Increase	Remain Static	Will Decrease
Turnover (net of inflation)	75	13	12	81	13	6
Share of Subcontracted Business in Turnover	19	67	14	23	69	8
Product/Service Range	61	34	15	56	40	4
Number of Customers	66	18	16	72	19	9
No. of outlets	30	56	14	43	49	8

Source: IMS/OSG Survey (Questions 2, 3 and 4)

*   Column 1 shows the extent of adoption in organisations in 1985/or change since 1983
    Column 2 shows the expected change in organisations over the period 1985 to 1990

Workforce Trends and Their Causes 1985-90

The case studies show that the trends towards infrastructure creation, internalisation of leisure and externalisation of cleaning and research services will continue. The picture emerging from the survey is optimistic: 81 per cent of the respondents expect the volume of their business to increase (Table 12.3c). The survey also indicates that new technologies and better working methods will continue to be taken on board (Tables 12.3a and 12.3b). Thus, employers in this sector expect both demand and productivity growth over the rest of this decade.

Demand growth, however, is expected to intensify especially in the three largest employment areas: hotels and catering; recreational services; and cleaning services. A more competitive exchange rate and an intensification in the overseas marketing activities are expected to ensure a strong growth in tourism. The main unknown factors are the volatility in the number of the American tourists abroad and the pace of improvement in the quality of management. The latter is a pre-requisite for the maturation of the industry under which seasonal and random fluctuations in demand are minimised. If US tourism grows and management continues to become more professional, the UK tourist industry is expecting an exceptional growth. The marketed recreational and cultural services, too, are expecting an intensification in the growth in demand as trends towards increased discretionary spending of both time and money, coupled with social trends towards greater participation in events outside the home, continue. Finally, cleaning services have yet to feel the full effects of the privatisation in the public sector. Coming on top of the continuing externalisation in the private sector, the industry is expecting buoyant demand at least until the end of this decade.

It is worth emphasising that the growth in demand will be organic in the first two industries and as such cause no direct noticeable displacement in other sectors. In contrast, that in cleaning services will be diversionary and be detrimental to jobs in other sectors, although numerically the growth in part-time jobs will exceed the decline in full-time jobs. Overall the sector's growth will, however, outstrip the accompanying productivity increases and result in the creation of jobs.

The assessments from the previous section show an expected increase in the sector's workforce over the rest of this decade. The results from the postal survey (Table 12.4) show that 51 per cent of the respondents expect their numbers to increase and 49 per cent expect a decrease. In the latter group, many respondents expect no more than a fractional decrease that is consistent with 'no change'. Where they are expected, the declines, on the whole, are likely in all employer size groups.

Table 12.4   Leisure and Related Services: Employment Growth to 1990
             Distribution of Respondents

Cumulative Employment Growth Band (per cent):	Sample Distribution (per cent)	Dominant Employer-Type*
less than -10	16	All
-9 to -5	5	All
-4 to 0	28	All
1 to 5	6	All
6 to 10	7	Small/Medium
Over 10	38	Small/Medium

*   This indicates the types of employer dominating the result in the previous column. Based on their employment numbers, four employer-types have been designated for this purpose: **Large** (over 500); **Medium** (200-499); **Small** (under 200); **All** (no dominance by size)

Source: IMS/OSG Survey (Question 5A)

When these estimates are combined with those from the case studies (covering many large firms), it emerges that the sector's workforce is expected to grow at an average of 2.4 per cent per annum over the rest of this decade. Nearly 300,000 additional jobs are expected to be created from a total of 2.66 million in 1985 to reach a total of nearly three million in 1990, with a variability margin of $\pm 100,000$ (Table 12.5). The occupational changes associated with this forecast are given in Part C.

There are a number of important features about these totals. First, self-employment will continue to grow but at a reduced rate. This is partly because its growth in the recent past was due to an exceptional economy-wide changes in 1980-81 and partly because larger employers will be establishing themselves across a wide area of the sector as part of their diversification strategies. Second, the pattern of employment growth will be uneven between industries. Personal services, for example, are unlikely to show much growth for reasons mentioned above. Third, according to the survey evidence, growth will favour female, part-time and young employees. In other words, employment growth will continue to favour the same employee groups, as in the past: namely, those who are new entrants to the labour market.

Table 12.5   Leisure and Other Services' Workforce: 1985-1990

SIC Class:		(thousands)		Annual Percentage Change
		1985	1990	
66,97	Leisure	1,468	1,605	+2.1
67,92 94,98	Other Services	728	788	+1.8
	Total Employment	2,196	2,393	+2.0
	Self-Employment	467	560	+4.4
	Total Workforce	2,663	2,953	+2.4

Source: IMS/OSG Survey and Case Studies

Summary

This Chapter has analysed the past and prospective trends in the workforce of the leisure and other services sector. Most of these services are supplied outside the public sector.

The sector's workforce has grown, since 1979, by 370,000: 140,000 through direct employment, and 230,000 through self-employment. The increase has been confined to hotels, catering, cleaning and R&D services. The upward trend evident in the last decade in sports and recreational services halted temporarily in recent years because of the indirect effects of the cash limits in public spending.

The increase in employment has come about largely through three factors: creation of new capacity in restaurant and fast food areas; growth in tourism; and the trend towards externalisation of cleaning and specialist functions on the part of other sectors. As a result, employment growth is part organic and part a redistribution between sectors. Another feature of the increase is that it has benefited the young, and female and part-time employees. Underlying this growth pattern, however, there have been a number of influences - technological as well as organisational - which are gradually rendering the sector less labour intensive.

Over the period to 1990, all these factors will endure. If anything, business growth is expected to accelerate and also become more broadly based. The business outlook for tourist, sports, recreational and cleaning services is seen as very favourable. Tourism is, of course, subject to the vagaries of the international market but the industry has prepared itself for strong growth. Accordingly, both employment and self-employment in the sector are expected to grow. From a base of 2.6 million in 1985, the workforce is expected to expand annually at an average of 2.4 per cent, generating an additional 300,000 jobs by the beginning of 1990: 200,000 through employment and 100,000 through self -employment. The overall variability margin is $\pm$100,000. Following the past pattern, the new jobs will mainly accrue to the new entrants to the labour. market - the young and part-time females.

13 Public Services

Background

The public sector lends itself to many definitions. The 1980 Standard Industrial Classification presents it under four categories: public administration and defence, education, health and welfare services. The armed forces are separately listed. There are also private and voluntary providers in education, health and welfare which, although growing, still constitute relatively minor sources of employment. The dominant influence on employment levels is the Government, directly as the employer of Civil Servants and the armed forces, and less directly as the prime force determining the financial provision and hence employment levels of the health service and the local authorities. Because of the dominant role of public finance and national policy in determining overall employment levels the analyses for this sector focused on an assessment of the Government's stated priorities and a series of detailed interviews with representatives in the main employing groups together with an assessment of secondary sources.

There are four main employer groups in the sector: the local authorities, the national health service, the civil service and the armed forces. Combined, as well as individually, they comprise the largest employers in the country. Total employment in the sector is just over five million and is spread across a number of major activities (Table 13.1). The sector is a major employer of part-time staff and of women who accounted for 33 per cent and 64 per cent respectively of the totals in 1985.

Table 13.1   Public Services: Activity Composition and Employment in 1985

SIC Class/Activity:		Employment in 1985	
		Numbers (thousands)	Percentage
91	**Public Administration and Defence**		
9117	National Government	395	8
9112	Local Government Services	600	12
9120	Justice	51	1
9130	Police	191	4
9140	Fire Services	61	1
9150	National Defence	123	2
9190	Social Security	100	2
93	**Education**	1,536	31
95	**Health**		
9510	Hospitals, Nursing Homes	1,060	21
9520	Other Medical Care Institutions	134	3
9530	Medical Practices	63	1
9540	Dental Practices	38	1
9550	Other Health Services	22	1
96	**Welfare and Other Services**	636	12
Total		5,010	100
(Armed Forces		327	-)

Source: Employment Gazette, December 1985

Until 1979, public sector employment had been on a long term growth pattern. Since then, there has been a reduction in numbers in two areas - public administration, and education - while health and welfare services have continued to experience an increase in employment (Table 13.2). Overall there was a small increase between 1979 and 1985.

Employment Trends and Their Causes to 1985

In a longer term context, 1979 was a watershed as the then new Government initiated a generalised reduction in the size and scope of public sector activities. The process has affected each of the main employer groups in different ways. Each is considered separately below.

Table 13.2   Public Services: Evolution of Employment 1979-85

(thousands)

SIC Class:	1979	1981	1985	Average Percentage Change 1979-85
91 Public Administration and Defence	1,671	1,575	1,521	-1.5
93 Education	1,590	1,546	1,536	-0.6
95 Medical and Health Services	1,186	1,243	1,317	+1.8
96 Welfare and Other Services	519	560	636	+3.8
Total	4,966	4,924	5,010	under +0.1
(Armed Forces	320	334	327	+0.3)

Source: Employment Gazette, Historical Supplement No 1, April 1985; and December 1985.

Tight cash limits and detailed staff review exercises have served to reduce **central government manpower** (civil servants) from 730,000 in the fiscal year 1979 to 620,000 in 1985. The decline has been borne by both industrial (blue collar) and non industrial (white collar) civil servants. The decline has occurred for several reasons: the introduction of new working practices, including greater delegation of functions to achieve greater job loading; fewer hierarchical layers; changes to the services provided; and the introduction of new technologies in areas such as typing pools and stores management, and particularly the administration of social and welfare benefits. Part of the reduction has also involved re-distribution of jobs from the public to the private sector rather than elimination as subcontracting has been undertaken in a number of areas such as catering, cleaning, computer work, security, accounting and printing, and others have been privatised. Although the general thrust has been towards a reduction in employment; not all departments have been subject to cuts. Exceptions include the Manpower Services Commission and the Home Office; in both cases the increases are due to policy measures in response to rising unemployment and an increased commitment to law and order.

A similar downward trend has been apparent in **local government manpower**; a reduction of around one per cent per annum since 1979. Here, too, tight cash limits have led to privatisation of certain services, the introduction of labour saving technologies - especially in office areas - improved working practices and changed service provision; for example, less frequent maintenance and cleaning. In the case of privatisation, by 1985 for example, 200 of out 536 local authorities had privatised one or more of the following functions: parks management, cleaning, refuse disposal, catering, street cleaning, car parks, window cleaning and pest control. In education the fall in employment prompted by falling the school rolls due to demographic factors affected both professional and support staff. As in central government, not all activities have been subject to cuts. Recent legislation on planning, community care, the Youth Training Scheme, unified housing benefits and the urban programme have led to a step increase in headcount by one per cent, while a growing demand for social service provision has expanded employment in that area. The pattern of change has not, however, been uniform between authorities.

In the **National Health Service** the demand for services has continued to grow and with it the reliance on central government finance. The main policy emphasis has been to increase staff providing medical services and to constrain the growth in support functions. New technologies have had a variable impact, reducing needs in the office and stores and laundry areas, or enabling service provision to increase without a consequent rise in support staff; while in some of the medical areas the use of new technology has increased the demand for staff such as technicians for analytical work. A growing emphasis on community care, and a transfer of some local health services from the NHS to local authorities, have meant there has also been a shift of employment between different parts of the public sector. Lastly, as with central government and the local authorities, there has been a growing emphasis on competitiveness tendering involving in-house departments and sub-contracting for services including cleaning and catering. In a number of authorities in-house departments are 'winning' the contracts for these

124

services but the pressure of competition is causing many in-house departments to change working methods and reduce employment levels.

Finally, public policy has been to strengthen the **armed forces,** and total numbers have increased slightly since 1979 although more recently a growing proportion of expenditure has been focused on the equipment budget.

There is also one general observation that concerns the female and part-time employees. As in other service industries, their share of employment has grown in the public services, primarily in the medical, health and welfare services (Table 13.3). This is principally related to the expansion of employment in occupations such as nursing and social welfare where there is a high usage of part-time employees to cover fluctuating work loads, and where there is traditionally a high density of female staff.

Table 13.3   Public Services: Pattern of Job Changes Between 1979 and 1985

SIC Activity:	Growth in 1979-85 in:		
	(thousands)		
	Total Employment	Female Employment	Part-time Employment
91 Public Administration and Defence	-150	- 87	- 26
93 Education	- 54	- 45	+ 51
95 Medical and Health Services	+131	+126	+105
96 Welfare and Other Services	+117	+105	+ 82
Total	+ 44	+ 99	+212

Source: Employment Gazette, February 1986

Employment Trends and Their Causes 1985-90

The interviews with individual employers in the different sectors, together with an assessment of public policy statements, formed the basis for the employment forecasts to 1990 (Table 13.4). Taking individual employer categories, Government policy is to reduce the number of civil servants to

590,000 by 1988 and, based on past evidence, this figure is likely to be achieved and may even be exceeded. The underlying causes are expected to be a continuation of the factors prevailing since 1979, including improved **work organisation, changed service provision, use of new technologies, and sub-contracting and privatisation.** This reduction is in part an inter sectoral shift due to contracting out services and the privatisation of activities such as dockyards. In the local authorities, the expectation is of a flat or slightly declining employment level brought about as a result of several divergent trends. In social services in particular, total employment is expected to grow alongside increased service provision, as will provision in several numerically smaller employment areas such as law and order. In other areas, a continued financial squeeze will continue to lead to reduction in manning levels through improved work organisation, changed service provision and the continued introduction of new technologies in the office areas. Further contracting out of services is also expected although this will result in an inter sectoral transfer. The contraction in education will continue as the school population continues to fall until 1990. In the national health service, a pattern of overall headcount growth is expected, again in response to **increased service provision,** with the moderating factors of contracting out, the use of new technologies and changed working practices reducing employment in many areas.

The main determinant of overall employment levels in the Public Sector will continue to be government policy and financial provision. Any change as a result of the general election which will have taken place by 1988 could have an impact on the figures for 1990. Another important variability will be the proportion of jobs filled by part-time workers (see below). Total employment is, however, expected to fall marginally by 60,000 by 1990, from a total of just over five million in 1985.

The variability around these forecasts is potentially large and has been assessed at $\pm$100,000 jobs. Within these totals the proportion and number of part-time jobs is expected to continue to grow, particularly in education where part-time staff for lunchtime supervision in schools are expected to be introduced instead of teachers fulfilling this role; and in health and welfare services, where there will be a growing use of part-time 'caring' staff. Different authorities will, however, pursue different policies in the staffing of many areas susceptible to part-time employment; this could affect the overall headcount totals as many operate their staffing levels in terms of 'Whole Time Equivalents'. The implications of the above developments for occupations are given in Part C of this report.

Table 13.4   Public Services Employment 1985-90

SIC Class:	(thousands)		Average Percentage Change 1985-90
	1985	1990	
91 Public Administration and Defence	1,521	1,460	-0.9
93 Education	1,536	1,450	-1.2
95 Medical and Health Services	1,317	1,350	+0.5
96 Welfare and Other Services	636	700	+2.2
Total	5,010	4,950	-0.2
(Armed Forces	327	325	-)

Source: IMS/OSG Interviews and The Government's Expenditure Plans
        (Cmnd. 9702-II)

Summary

This chapter has examined the past and prospective evolution of employment in
public services. In the last decade, it increased consistently in response to
social, economic and political influences. However, since 1979 the trend has
been reversed in areas involving administration and support activities, and
eased in those involving the provision of services such as health and welfare
while education has continued to decline. The changes have occurred in part in
response to the Government's declared objective of reducing the scope and size
of the public sector. This has involved the contracting out of certain
services.

Previously provided in-house; introduction of new technologies; and the
reorganisation of work and services. It has in part been due to demographic
and social trends. These factors are likely to continue over the rest of the
decade with employment associated with education and administration declining

and slow expansion in medical and welfare services employment. From a level of over five million, the sector is expected to contract its employment by 60,000 by 1990. However, the associated variability in the forecast is exceptionally wide because of its sensitivity to public policy, and the scope for employers substituting full and part-time jobs.

14 Small Firms

Background

Small firms have featured prominently in the public discussions on areas of
new jobs in the future - both in the UK and other OECD countries. Yet at
detailed level, there still remains notable gaps in knowledge on aspects of
employment and occupations associated with small firms. A substantive theme
emerging from the employment forecasts in the previous ten Chapters is that
growth in employment over the rest of this decade is expected to be more
widespread among smaller rather than larger employers. However, the definition
of smaller employers adopted so far in the study has not been precise. It has
encompassed independent firms as well as work establishments or branches of
larger firms. This has been inevitable because it has not been possible to
ascertain the exact corporate status of all the organisations involved.

To obtain a sharper focus on independent small firms a three-stage approach
has been adopted: an extensive literature survey covering the UK and other
countries; consultations with experts on small firms; and a detailed special
survey of small firms which involved interviews with 298 small firms. This
part of the study was carried out in conjunction with a group of specialists
in small firms research. The main features are described in Chapter 3. This
Chapter summarises the main results from this extensive part of the work
programme.

The small firms survey involving 298 firms, had a wide geographical spread in
order to capture the inter-regional variety in labour market and economic
characteristics in the UK. Beyond that, it also tried to replicate, as far as
possible, the national industrial distribution of small firms, as recorded by
the latest (1981) VAT Register at the time of the survey in May 1985. The
adopted definition of a small firm is one with a turnover of under £1,000,000
in manufacturing and £250,000 in other sectors (in 1981 prices). On this

definition, the industrial distribution of the sample relates to that provided by the VAT Register (Table 14.1). It should be borne in mind that these firms overlap with sectoral coverage in the previous Chapters.

Table 14.1   Industrial Distribution of Small Firms

(percentages)

Industrial Group:	VAT Register	IMS Small Firms Survey
Manufacturing	13	17
Construction	15	9
Transport Services	4	2
Wholesaling and Dealing	7	5
Retail Distribution	25	30
Finance	6	6
Catering	12	9
Motor Trades	6	7
Other Services	12	15
Total	100	100

Source: VAT Register and IMS/OSG Small Firms Survey

Apart from its wide industrial coverage, the survey also achieved a fair cross-section in terms of two key characteristics: employment-size and age of business. The sampled firms had varying number of employees: some had only one, others had more than 20. Collectively, the sampled firms had 2,069 employees (Table 14.2). In terms of their age distribution there is again a wide cross-section, with well defined extremes: 10 firms had been in business for less than a year and 62 firms for over 25 years. Such diversity is essential in order to establish whether new jobs are coming from new-starts or established firms (Table 14.3).

This gives the background of the survey. The next two sections look at the factors affecting the growth and occupational structure of these small firms and attempts to answer three broad questions:

a.   How many new jobs have been created by the sampled firms over the period 1980-85, and what are the underlying causes?

b. How many new jobs are likely to be created over the rest of this
   decade, and what are the underlying causes?

c. How and why are their occupational structures changing?

Table 14.2   Employment Structure of Sampled Firms in 1985

Number of Employees	Number of Firms	% of Total	Number of Employees	% of Total
1	24	8	24	1
2	57	19	114	6
3	42	14	126	6
4	48	16	192	9
5	23	8	115	6
6	27	9	162	8
7-10	32	11	267	13
11-20	29	10	405	20
Over 20	16	5	664	32
Total	298	100	2,069	100

Source: IMS/OSG Small Firms Survey

Table 14.3   Age Structure of Sampled Firms in 1985

Age of Firm	Number of Firms*	% of Total	Employment	% of Total
Less than 1 year	10	3)		
1 year	23	8)		
2 years	21	7)	509	25
3 years	24	8)		
4 years	25	8)		
5 years	20	7)	464	23
6-10 years	38	13)		
11-24 years	69	24	432	21
Over 25 years	62	21	627	31

* Six firms gave no details regarding the age of the business.

Source: IMS/OSG Small Firms Survey

The resulting assessment, together with the analysis of previous research and data, then forms the basis of the nationwide forecasts of job creation by small firms.

Employment Generation in Period 1980-85

Before examining the scale and composition of new jobs created by small firms, it is important to examine the reasons that have underpinned the formation of small firms in the survey (Table 14.4). It emerges that there is no single over-riding factor. Although unemployment or fear of it is cited most frequently, there are others which are reported to be of similar importance, once allowance is made for the inevitable overlapping causes. For example social and personal factors are just as important as the economic ones.

Table 14.4   Main Reasons for Setting Up in Business

Reason	Number of Firms	Percentage of Total
Saw market need/had good idea/desire for profit	32	12
Unemployment or threatened unemployment	38	15
Desire for independence from employer	34	13
Connections with family or friends	32	12
Knowledge of, or interest in, trade	33	13
Long standing ambition to own business	11	4
'Opportunity arose'/other reason	17	6
Took over established firm	19	7
Previously in business	18	7
Long established firm	27	10
(No information given)	(37)	-
Total	298	100

Source: IMS/OSG Small Firms Survey

Table 14.3 showed that the sample is an amalgam of firms established before 1980 and new-starts since then. It is clear that jobs have been created in both groups. As Table 14.5 shows, firms established before 1980 have created 205 new jobs; implying an annual growth of four per cent in this decade. When these estimates are combined with those associated with new starts, it emerges that the annual job creation is around 14 per cent. However, this is a vast **over-estimate** because the sample perforce excludes established firms who had ceased trading at the time of the survey. For example, according to the VAT Register, 10 per cent of **all** businesses cease to trade each year. More importantly, death rates are particularly high amongst young and small firms: on average over 40 per cent of new firms cease to trade within two and a half years of start-up (Ganguly, 1985). Hence, the figure of 14 per cent needs to be scaled down substantially.

Another notable feature of the results in Table 14.5 is that growth in employment has been accompanied by certain compositional changes: the **share** of female and part-time employees has increased and that of full-time male decreased. More significantly, the increase in the share of part-time employees between 1980 and 1985 masks the notable differences between the two types of firms. Female part-time labour provided 28 per cent of new jobs in the established firms and 19 per cent in the new firms. In other words, new-starts favoured male and full-time employees.

Table 14.5   Small Firms: Growth in Employment

Types of Firm:	Number of Employees in	
	1980	1985
Established Firms	1,029	1,234*
New Firms		509
Total	1,029	1,743
Percentage Share of:		
Female and Part-time	16	19
Full-time Male	56	51

* Excludes 18 established firms who could not provide the estimates for 1980, their employment in 1985 was 326.

Source: IMS/OSG Small Firms Survey

Finally, the survey also sought to establish the occupational background of employment in 1985. As is well known, a characteristic feature of small firms is the extreme flexibility in functions and job titles. Thus any occupational breakdown can be no more than illustrative. As Table 14.6 shows, the largest group comprise managers, administrators and professionals, most of whom are the owners of the firms. Beyond that, there was no clear bias in favour of any specific group. Nor has the distribution changed much since 1980 amongst the established firms. Such changes as have been recorded in this group appear to favour occupations at the level of operatives and below. Of course, a breakdown by different industries would reveal a pronounced variability in occupational patterns. But the sample size is not large enough to warrant detailed industry-specific observations; nor are the occupational titles clearly defined within small firms.

Table 14.6   Small Firms: Occupational Structure of the Workforce in 1985

Occupation:	Percentage Distribution
Management, Administration Professional and Technical	30
Craftsmen	20
Operatives	24
Support and Personal Services	21
Others	5
Total	100

Source: IMS/OSG Small Firms Survey

The recent growth in employment and some of its compositional characteristics have been shown above. Three broad areas of the firms' operations are now considered in order to understand the background against which growth has occurred. They are: business aspects, use of new technologies, and working methods.

Taking them in turn, it emerges from the analysis that an increase in the volume of turnover has been widespread: 62 per cent of the respondents had experienced an increase and 16 per cent a decrease. The increase had been underpinned by an enhancement in product/service range, customer-base and productive capacity. Significantly, there has been much less reliance on exports and subcontracting to other firms (Table 14.7). Hence, the first implication is that employment growth has emanated from **domestic business** and has involved **capacity expansion.** The evidence from the small firms suggest that business growth in small firms has emanated from three sources: discovery of new market niches; subcontracting by larger firms; and displacement of business outside the small firms sector through greater competition. As such business growth has involved a significant redistributive element between categories of firms.

Table 14.7   Small Firms' Business Aspects 1982-84

Business Aspect:	Number of Firms Responding	(percentages)		
		Increased	Remained Static	Decreased
Volume of Turnover	245	62	22	16
Share of Exports in Output	36*	33	61	6
Product/Service Range	223	48	44	7
Customer Base	237	48	39	13
Volume of Subcontracted Business	64	34	56	9
Productive Capacity	160	48	46	6

* The low responses here reflect the low proportion of small firms involved in export related activities.

Source: IMS/OSG Small Firms Survey

As for the use of new technologies, the scale of their adoption has been negligible: less than 10 per cent of the respondents had introduced new technologies on a large scale. This applies to all functions which are amenable to technological changes: namely, office work, production, bought-in components, storage and distribution (Table 14.8). Thus, the second implication is that, contrary to popular belief, small firms - both established and new starts - do not regard themselves as innovators in respect of the use of technology.

Table 14.8   Small Firms: Introduction of New Technologies, 1982-84

Function:	Number of Firms Responding	(Percentages)		
		Large Extent	Limited Extent	Negligible
Office Functions	214	8	16	76
Possible Processes	149	9	20	72
Components etc	156	6	18	76
Storage etc	147	5	11	84

Source: IMS/OSG Small Firms Survey

Finally, and as a corollary of business growth, working methods have become more efficient in many small firms. Between 30 and 50 per cent of the respondents have secured improvements in the quality of equipment, premises and management and in labour productivity (Table 14.9). Indeed, the comparative advantage of the sampled firms appeared to be in these areas. The flexibility with which they have been able to implement changes has been an important element of their survival mechanism and growth. But the point needs to be put into context: over 50 per cent had experienced no changes in any aspect of their working methods. So the third implication is that improvements in working methods are occurring but their incidence is not so comprehensive.

Table 14.9   Small Firms: Working Methods 1982-84

Aspects of Method:	Number of Firms Responding	(Percentages)		
		Improved	Same	Worse
Equipment	250	52	46	2
Premises	253	38	60	2
Labour Utilisation	235	28	70	2
Management Performance	226	40	58	2

Source: IMS/OSG Small Firms Survey

To summarise employment growth in the established small firms has averaged around four per cent per annum in this decade. It has disproportionately benefited female and part-time employees. Although improvements within the firm have helped, growth has relied heavily on home demand.

Employment Trends and Their Causes 1985-90

The evidence in Tables 14.10 to 14.12 indicate that the critical determinant of employment in the medium term will continue to be the state of demand rather than improvements in working methods or the introduction of new technologies. For example, less than 10 per cent of the respondents expect to adopt new technologies on a 'large extent'. This is also substantially corroborated by the evidence emerging from the 'open-ended' part of the discussion schedule, which sought to identify the main influences on future employment. The results (Table 14.12) show that 'market demand' received just over 25 per cent of the mentions and business factor under 25 per cent. The two are, of course, inter-related. Surprisingly perhaps, the factors often highlighted in the public discussion - e.g. red tape/regulations, Government policy - received relatively few mentions.

Table 14.10   Small Firms: Business Aspects 1985-90

(percentages)

Business Aspects:	Number of Firms Responding	Likely to Increase	Likely to Remain Static	Likely to Decrease
Volume of Turnover	273	71	18	11
Share of Exports in Output	38*	47	47	5
Product/Service Range	256	46	47	7
Customer Base	271	57	35	8
Volume of Sub-Contracted Business	70	37	51	11
Productive Capacity	167	50	42	7

*   The low responses here reflect the low proportion of small firms involved in export related activities.

Source: IMS/OSG Small Firms Survey

Table 14.11   Small Firms: Technological Change 1985-90

(percentages)

Functions:	Number of Firms Responding	Large Extent	Limited Extent	Negligible
Office Functions	239	7	25	68
Production Processes	154	8	25	70
Components etc	166	4	27	69
Storage etc	158	4	20	77

Source: IMS/OSG Small Firms Survey

Table 14.12   Factors Influencing Employment Change

Factor:	Number of Mentions	Percentage of Mentions
a. Market demand	104	27
b. General economic climate	20	5
c. Business factors	88	23
d. Competition/competitiveness	23	6
e. Government policies	8	2
f. Regulations/red tape	11	3
g. Cost of rent and/or rates	17	5
h. Employment costs and/or problems	14	4
i. Growth unlikely	27	7
j. Miscellaneous local factors	27	7
k. Other factors	41	11
Total	381	100

Source: IMS/OSG Small Firms Survey

As for employment forecasts, of the 298 respondents, only 176 could offer estimates of their employment to 1990. Taking 176 firms as a base, their qualitative pattern of growth was as follows:

	Per Cent
Employment likely to increase	40
Employment likely to remain static	53
Employment likely to decrease	7

Translated into headcount, the firms expect an increase of 259 jobs from a base of 1,033 in 1985, giving an annual rate of growth of six per cent. This rate is higher than that experienced in the past five years by the firms existing in 1980. However, two caveats are necessary.

First, nearly 40 per cent of the survey respondents could not offer a prediction. This is indicative of the uncertain climate in which most small firms operate. Second, the youngest firms tended to be most optimistic; yet their vulnerability is only too well known. For example, out of the 259 extra jobs expected by the end of this decade, 99 (38 per cent) are expected to be created in firms which are less than five years old. Past evidence suggests that this group has the highest mortality rate. For example, more than half the firms born in 1983 are unlikely to be in existence in 1989 (Ganguly, 1985). The projected six per cent growth therefore needs to be scaled down.

Table 14.13   Small Firms' Occupational Structure: 1985-90

(percentages)

Occupation:	1985	1990
Managers and Administrators	25	23
Engineers, Scientists, Technologists	2	2
Other Professions	3	3
Technicians and Draughtsmen	1	1
Craftsmen and	18	18
Operatives	22	25
Support Services	14	12
Personal Services	8	7
Others	7	9
Total	100	100

Source: IMS/OSG Small Firms Survey

Before deriving the grossed up estimates, two features of the forecasts given above need mentioning. First, a disproportionate number of jobs are expected to be full- rather than part-time. Whereas part-time employment represented 29 per cent of the (predicting) firms' employment in 1985, only 14 per cent of their new jobs will be part-time. Thus there is an expectation that the past trend towards part-time employment will be reversed or eased over the rest of this decade. Second, the occupational structure is likely to change, as can be seen in Table 14.13. While the shares of managers and support personnel are likely to decline, that of operatives are expected to increase. The shift is indicative of the process of organic growth in established firms. Their additional employment does not call for more managers, since in most cases owners themselves are managers.

So much for the unadjusted forecasts resulting from the small firms survey. So far, one salient point that stands out above all else is that forecasting employment in small firms is unusually difficult because of high birth and high death rates. Hence, in order to forecast employment and occupational structure in small businesses in five years' time, critical judgements have to be made on the following aspects:

a. numbers and characteristics of the existing firms which will cease to exist by 1990;

b. numbers and types of firms which are not yet in existence, but which will be trading in 1990; and

c. the validity of the forecasts provided by those who expect to survive, in the light of either their past employment performance or their future business expectations.

Clearly, the uncertainty in each of these areas argues for a variable forecast, associated with three distinct assumptions:

Case 1: recent trends in the birth and the death rates of small firms will continue until 1990.

Case 2: there will be a 10 per cent increase in the birth rate, but resulting in a 50 per cent displacement of the existing small firms. In other words, there will be a net increase in the population of small firms over and above the historical rate of growth of small firms.

Case 3: there will be a 10 per cent increase in the birth rate, but resulting in a 100 per cent displacement of existing firms, with the result that there will be no increase over and above the historical growth rate in the small firms' population.

The displacement possibilities implied by Cases 2 and 3 are confined to the small firms' population. However, following the recent pattern all three cases are also expected to cause displacement outside the small firms sector.

Forecasts have been constructed for each of these cases by combining the survey results with the published data on population, births and deaths of small firms. Here only the summary findings are presented.

Table 14.14 gives the results for each case under two assumptions - one optimistic and one less so. The optimistic one is that the future projections emerging from the survey will materialise. The second one is that the future growth in small firms will be in line with recent growth; the latter has been lower than the former. In other words, the first assumption argues that the optimistic forecasts of the survey are warranted. The second assumption is that future growth will be as in the past.

The results are therefore presented in the form of six variants. The choice between cases has to be a matter of personal judgement. The substantive point to note is that the size of the workforce in the small firms sector was estimated to be 5.0 million in 1985 according to British Business (22 November 1985). The results in the table show that by 1990 it could rise to a minimum of 5.7 million (Case 1, past trends) or a maximum of 6.3 million (Case 2, future projections).

Put simply, these projections mean that small firms are expected to increase their employment by:

a.   an additional 700,000 jobs if recent trends in job creation and new births and deaths continue over the rest of this decade. The analysis of previous research and consultations with sector experts indicate that this is the most likely scenario;

or

b.   an additional 1.24 million jobs if the optimistic forecasts on job creation by the small firms are borne out, together with a net increase in the rate of start-ups such that the number of new jobs created, by new starts exceeds the number displaced in the established small firms.

In either case these figures focus on changes in employment in small firms. They do not represent the net increases in the overall workforce but rather a change in the relative share as some of the jobs gained have been due to organic growth others have come via subcontracting, or indirectly, from larger firms.

Table 14.14   Forecasts with Different Cases to 1990*

	Assumptions	Continuation of Recent Trends	Small Firms' Own Projections
		(thousands)	
Case 1:	Continuation of past trends in births and deaths	5,690	6,120
Case 2:	A 10 per cent increase in birth rate with 50 per cent displacement in established small firms	5,840	6,260
Case 3:	A 10 per cent increase in birth rate with 100 per cent displacement in established small firms	5,700	6,140

*   The 1985 estimate of employment is 5,020 (thousands)

Source: IMS/OSG Small Firms Survey

The occupational and compositional elements associated with these extremes are, of course, different. At the lower extreme, the occupational structure will tend to remain as shown in Table 14.13. The main beneficiary would be the operatives and part-time female employees. However, in the case of the upper extreme, the figures become dominated by new-starts who tend to employ more of two groups: full-time employees; and managers and higher level occupations, the latter reflecting the background of the owners.

Finally all three cases are expected to produce job displacement outside the small firms sector, following the past pattern. Whereas its extent is difficult to quantify it is expected to be substantial.

Summary

This Chapter has had a narrow focus: namely, small independent firms - both long established and new-starts. It has summarised the results of detailed parallel study designed to assess the potential for new jobs in such firms over the rest of this decade. The scale of their job creation in the past is not easy to establish because of a high incidence of corporate births and deaths. Amongst the firms established before 1980 and still trading in 1985, and covered in the survey, the rate has averaged an annual four per cent. The figure is indicative and not definitive. Whatever the precise figure, growth has been led by home rather than export demand, according to the surveyed firms. They attach only a relatively low importance to the use of new technologies or improved working methods in respect of their employment growth.

The main point emerging from this Chapter is that small firms will be creating jobs in most sectors at a time when large firms are expected to reduce them, in part through transferance to smaller firms. Over the rest of this decade, the potential for more job creation has been identified; its scale is, however, exceptionally uncertain because of three unknowns: the birth rate, the death rate, and the reliability of the employment projections emerging from this part of the study; all of which are indicative of the difficult environment in which small firms operate.

As a result, the projections are highly variable. They suggest that small firms who currently employ just over 5 million people may generate between 0.7 to 1.24 million new jobs over the period to 1990. Employment growth is expected to emanate from three sources: organic growth in business based on discovery of new market opportunities; subcontracting by larger firms; and displacement of jobs in the latter, through a competitive effect. As such, a large part of growth in employment is expected to be redistributive from other sectors to small firms. The lower end of the range is expected to be the most likely possibility, it assumes that recent trends in job creation, birth rate and death rate will continue in the future. The higher end assumes an intensification in the rates of both job creation and new births. In both cases these figures do not represent a net increase in the total workforce but rather a change in the share taken by small firms.

The lower forecast suggests that there will be relatively better prospects for two employee groups: part-time female and operatives. This is because growth will emanate from both new-starts and established firms. The latter tend to favour such groups. At the upper end, the prospects of two groups are likely to be better; full-time male, and managerial and professional groups. This is because new-starts usually use such groups in the capacity of owners of small firms or their family members.

Part C : Whole Economy

The previous eleven Chapters have assessed the job prospects in each of the specified sectors. As such, they have concentrated on two aspects: the **industrial** background and the causes underlying the changes in organisations employment levels. Both aspects constitute essential building blocks for constructing a picture of the workforce in the whole economy over the rest of this decade.

Such a picture is an essential pre-requisite for understanding the trends in the qualitative aspects of the workforce which have thus far remained in the background. The main aspects in this context are job status, age, sex and occupations.

Accordingly, this part of the report constructs an **aggregate** picture and highlights the **qualitative** aspects and the factors underlying the changes. In this process, it also brings out a number of issues which have not been covered as yet because either they have an economy-wide impact, or they specifically concern the qualitative aspects.

There are three Chapters in this part. The first constructs an aggregate picture and describes some of the qualitative aspects of changes in the workforce. These serve to pave the way towards assessing the key occupational trends in the next Chapter and the consequences for skills in the last Chapter. Throughout, reference is made to the main factors employers expect to underly these changes.

15 Total Workforce To 1990

Issues

Part B set out employers' expectations of future trends in the size of the workforce in individual sectors and the underlying causes. This Chapter draws the trends together in order to derive an aggregate picture of the workforce to 1990. In the process, it also covers three aspects which have not been fully covered before: the role of certain general factors, that are not necessarily sector-specific, but have an economy-wide impact; the changing compositional elements of the workforce; and comparison of the IMS/OSG forecasts with those from other sources. The chapter seeks to answer the following questions:

(a) What are the key factors underlying the forecasts?

(b) What is the expected size of the economy's workforce by the end of this decade?

(c) What are the expected changes in its age, sex and part-time composition and the underlying causes?

(d) What are the differences between these forecasts and those derived and published by others?

Before tackling these questions, a general observation is necessary. The forecasts emerging from the previous Chapters are meant to be indicative of the **underlying** trends. They are based on the assumption made by employers participating in this study that the economy will grow at between 2-3 per cent per annum - a figure that is broadly in line with the prevailing stance of the national economic policy. However, in so far as there may be major policy changes or indeed abnormal developments like a **lasting** drop in the price of oil, their potential effects are accommodated as far as possible by offering a range associated with the forecasts. For example, if the policy stance becomes distinctly more expansionary and/or the price of oil remains at the existing low level over the rest of the decade, then the outcome is more likely to be at the upper-end of the range.

Factors Underlying the Workforce Changes to 1990

Before aggregating the projected changes in the workforce of individual sectors, it is worth summarising the factors that underpin them. These are drawn from the individual sectoral Chapters and presented in Table 15.1. It is clear that some factors are sector-specific as in the case of agriculture; whereas others apply across a number of sectors.

In the production industries (covering energy, manufacturing and construction), surplus capacity is expected to be the key influence on the projected size of the workforce. Even though an expansion in demand and output is expected across most of these industries, it is not expected to lead to an increase in workforce for three reasons. First, many of the case study firms reported that they still had surplus capacity; some of which was regarded as uneconomic despite the efficiency improvements that had been, and will continue to be made over the rest of the decade. Many firms expected to continue to close such capacity with a consequent reduction in employment. Second, in capital intensive areas considerable output growth is possible without the need to increase employment levels. Finally, in all areas the continuing application of new technologies and working methods are expected to generate significant producitivity increases which will absorb the growth in output. As such output growth will be either jobless or accompanied by further reductions in employment.

On the other hand, demand growth in service industries, is expected to generate new jobs. Here, too, new technologies and better working methods are expected to be applied but the resulting productivity growth is expected to be lower than the projected demand growth, emanating from the continuing externalisation of the service functions by other sectors, and the rising market penetration. Furthermore, if anticipated developments such as the reform of the Wages Councils and trading hours do materialise they will assist job creation, albeit on a small scale.

But the scale of overall job creation in services needs to be put into perspective. Leaving aside the inter-sectoral redistribution, the potential for organic growth in service employment is constrained by two factors. First, the exposure of service industries to foreign trade is limited because such trade is expected to remain highly protected, especially in areas like insurance, banking and professional services (Petit, 1986). If anything, the UK's share in this trade is declining (The Bank of England Bulletin, September 1985). Second, the scale of increase in services demand has to be very large for the employment effect to be significant. Or, as Sir John Harvey-Jones of the ICI argued in a slightly different context in this year's Richard Dimbleby lecture, if his company, ICI, went under 'you will need to entertain at least six million tourists each year, that is 40 per cent more than we now entertain'.

Another factor employers expect to affect the evolution of the workforce is the quality and culture of management. For example, nearly 70 per cent of the manufacturing firms in the IMS/OSG survey had recorded improvements in the calibre of management already in this decade; and 79 per cent are expecting further improvements. The respective figures for services are equally high. However, in the case studies, just as many expressed real concern at the existing shortcomings and the problems this would continue to pose over the rest of the decade unless there was a notable change. As one Chief Executive put it, 'our worst restrictive practices are those of conservative, poor quality management'. That apart, under recessionary pressures retrenchment and profitability were seen as more important than organic growth. That such an outlook prevails in many organisations is not open to doubt, and it is clearly not conducive to the generation of new jobs in the short term. On employers' own admissions, there is a need for a step improvement in management quality and a greater balance between profitability and growth. Significantly, in only one sector - retail distribution - were excessive wage increases regarded as a cause of low employment. Nobody approved of them; far from it. But they were accepted as inevitable in deference to the notions of 'fairness' and 'comparability'. Their root cause was perceived to be management inability to secure compensatory productivity gains. As a chief executive of one of the largest firms observed 'in this place, the gifted amateur reigns supreme'. The issue of management is considered futher in Chapter 17.

Thus both demand and supply side factors were regarded as essential for creating new jobs. They were perceived as requiring not only a growing economy and, particularly in the manufacturing sectors, increased competitiveness at home and abroad, but also greater investment in physical and human resources. This conclusion can perhaps best be illustrated by listing the features of firms who were expecting to increase their employment over the rest of this decade, irrespective of their industrial background. The relevance of the features varied between organisations and industries. The list is not definitive; nor does it constitute a rank order. In many cases, only one or two features prevailed; in others there were more but they were highly inter-related through a virtuous circle. They included:

o   ability to sell the 'know-how' as well as products;

o   specialised product lines and diversified customer-base;

o   a marked increase in turnover;

o   weakening job demarcations;

o   constant improvements in skills through regular training and recruitment of qualified manpower;

o   innovation in the adoption of technologies, product ideas and working methods.

o   increased competitiveness;

o   expansion in productive capacity;

Some Generalised Factors

Apart from the factors mentioned in Table 15.1, there are three other factors which have been perceived by many to have a high prominance and which have had either only a passing mention in the sectoral Chapters or none at all because their impact is expected to occur across a number of sectors, given their generalised nature. The factors in question are: mergers and corporate takeovers; special employment measures; and inward investment. Each are considered separately below.

Table 15.1   Factors Influencing Workforce Outlook to 1990: An Overview

Sectors:	Factors:
Primary Industries	
1. Agriculture, Forestry, Fishing	Restrictive stance of the EEC farm policy; falling farm incomes: and continuing 'industrialisation' of the farming methods.
2. Energy and Water Supply	Uneconomic/surplus capacity; increasing uncompetitiveness of coal; declining importance of energy-consuming industries; new technologies and better working methods.
Manufacturing	
3. Process Industries	Uneconomic/surplus capacity; declining importance of user industries; mergers; investment abroad; new technologies and better working methods.
4. Engineering and Related Industries	Demand growth uneven between industries; international uncompetitiveness; uneconomic/surplus capacity; continuing subcontracting; new technologies; flexible manning.
5. Light Production Industries	Demand growth uneven between industries; international uncompetitiveness; changing structure of retail trade; new technologies and better working methods.
Construction	
6. Construction	Improved growth prospects; but matched by higher productivity due to subcontracting of labour and material.
Services	
7. Distributive, Financial and Business Services	Growth in business due to subcontracting of services by other sectors and rising market penetration; new technologies; improved working methods; possible reform of Wages Councils and de-regulation of trading hours.
8. Transport and Communication	Business growth uneven between industries and offset by productivity growth in response to new technologies, improved working methods and growing competition.
9. Leisure and Other Services	Business growth due to subcontracting of services by other sectors; increased tourism and leisure activities; use of new technologies and better working methods improve productivity but not enough to offset business growth.
10. Public Service	Government expenditure plans, new technologies, contracting out of various functions.

Source: Chapters 4-13

a.   Mergers and Corporate Takeovers

Mergers and corporate takeovers in recent years have attracted considerable publicity because of their two features: the large size and the reliance on debt-finance. The case studies covering several recent mergers showed that their employment implications have involved job losses in the firms concerned of up to 20 per cent over a two year period. This applied to mergers involving vertical as well as horizontal integration. The reasons were two fold.

First, through the use of new technologies, the emerging organisational structures had become highly centralised, with increasing functional integration. This helped to eliminate duplication in the hierarchical structures as well as in head office functions. In insurance, finance and retailing, in some cases the elimination also extended to the branch and stores networks, where there had been overlaps. Second, the reliance on debt-finance generated cost pressures and the need for rapid reduction in headcounts, through either partial divestments or redundancies. For example, in one textile and clothing group, the merger resulted in a substantial restructuring, involving closure of two factories and a reduction of 18 per cent in the headcount in the first two years, as well as the divestment of the retail operations. Whether the resulting streamlined group had become more efficient or not was too soon to judge.

The substantive point is that the evolution of the workforce in the medium term is not dependent only on the supply and demand factors summarised in Table 15.1. Changes in the structure of corporate ownership are also a factor to consider. Should the current trend towards the so-called mega-mergers continue then there is every likelihood that the workforce size in 1990 will edge towards the lower end of the forecast range, presented in the next section. However, in so far as some of the mergers are also expected to improve the international trade performance of the companies covered, this will have a moderating effect.

b.   Special Employment Measures

In the last five years, five special employment measures involving the workforce have been introduced by the Government: Enterprise Allowance Scheme; Job Release Scheme; Young Workers Scheme; Youth Training Scheme and New Workers Scheme. The impact of the first four of these on future employment levels was considered in the case studies. The last one was introduced after the field work was complete.

It emerged that although they had been taken into account, their prospective impact was difficult for employers to quantify because of three factors. First, such measures usually have some 'deadweight' effect, resulting from a subsidy being paid for jobs which would have been created anyway. Second, the 'true' job creation element of the measures rests more on social than economic reasons and is thus largely influenced by the employers' degree of social responsibility, which they could not assess far into the future. Third, in so far as the reasons are economic, the measures will only have a long-term impact if they are operating for a period longer than has been the case in the past. This is because the financial incentives available under the measures take time to generate improved competitiveness, higher output and new jobs. Most of the special measures of the last ten years have had a time span of one to five years - a period not long enough in most cases for the competitive effect to feed into employment. Thus, whereas it was clear that the measures are expected to promote new jobs (net of deadweight), their numbers are unlikely to be so large that they could not be accommodated within the forecast range given in the next section. Their main impact is expected to be felt on the distribution of jobs between various categories of employees at whom the measures were targeted.

c.   Inward Investment

In recent years, there has been a notable increase in the number of new projects in the UK undertaken by foreign-owned firms - from 133 in 1982 to 317 in 1984. In part, companies are being attracted to the UK by access to European markets and, in the high-tech area, by the availability of skilled personnel. The associated job creation and job protection has increased four fold: from 10,500 to a high of 45,000 in 1984, according to the estimates compiled by the Invest in Britain Bureau.

However, before an assessment can be made of the impact of inward investment the relative importance of three kinds of employment effect associated with it have to be considered:

(a)   **macroeconomic effect**, resulting from the impact of an fresh injection of overseas funds into the UK's national income, balance of payments and Government revenue. In so far as the injection permits an expansionary government policy stance, domestic employment would be higher than it would otherwise have been;

(b)   **supportive effect,** resulting from the overseas-based firms displacing imports, generating exports or developing linkages with domestic enterprises, as the latter act as distributors or suppliers to the new entrants. Such outcomes have a benefical effect on UK employment;

(c)   **displacement effect,** resulting from the new entrants competing with domestic firms in the UK market and displacing existing employment through a loss of market share. The new entrants' employment creation is thus diversionary. The diversion is, of course, 100 per cent when the new entrants are merely taking over an indigenous firm.

Thus, all other things being equal, the first two kinds of effect will involve a level of employment higher than it would otherwise have been. The third effect, on the other hand, would be adverse, its extent being determined by the degree of domestic competition.

An assessment of the first kind of effect was not possible because it involves the use of a large-scale econometric model. However, an assessment was made of the other two effects for three industries: oil, electronics and banking. Their choice was influenced by three considerations: each has been a major recipient of inward investment in recent years; each has long established indigenous firms; each is highly diverse in its operations, products and customer-base.

The assessment suggests that in the case of the **oil** industry, the supportive effect has prevailed on the whole. This is because inward investment has been substantially directed at the North Sea, where capital costs are high and/or the indigenous firms have lacked the requisite technological know-how until recently.

In marked contrast, in **electronics** there has been a supportive effect in some cases as they have displaced imports and generated exports, but there has also been some displacement as foreign firms have taken an increasing share of the albeit expanding market to the detriment of the domestic firms. These companies have also been competing for the limited supply of scarce skills.

In **banking,** the effect was supportive until 1982. Overseas banks were mainly engaged in the Eurocurrency markets through collaborative ventures with the indigenous banks in order to pool the risk. Since then, however, they have increasingly ventured into wholesale and retail money business. One of the case study overseas-based banks has firm plans to open over 100 branches in the UK at a time when the domestic clearing banks will be further contracting their networks. As such, the inward investment in the past three years has had a growing displacement effect.

The experiences of these three industries do not provide a definitive assessment of the new jobs created by inward investment. Rather, they illustrate various possibilities with the aid of industry-specific examples. These prompt two observatons. First, if inward investment involves collaborative ventures, an infusion of special 'know-how' or displacement of imports then their job creation will be substantially free of displacement, as in the case of North Sea oil. Second, however, it is clear that a number of inward investment projects in recent years have been directed at traditional areas like retailing, catering, travel, and electronics where there are long-established indigenous firms. Here, some displacement will have occurred.

In the light of the recent statistics and the above observations, the forecasts that follow incorporate two assumptions. First, about 30,000 additional jobs a year are likely to be associated with inward investment through four routes: acquisition, expansion, joint venture and new company starts; with about half of these jobs likely to materialise through the last route. Second, a significant proportion, possibly up to a half, will involve displacement. Even if displacement is assumed to be lower, the extent of job creation from inward investment will, however, be low in relation to the overall size of the workforce.

If there seems to have been a disproportionate space allocated to this phenomenon, this is intentional for two contrasting reasons. First, the media attention on projects like the Nissan factory and McDonalds hamburgers operations have suggested that inward investment is a major nationwide phenomenon. Secondly, not withstanding the size of its contribution, inward investment is a source of new jobs in the economy, and is particularly beneficial to the host localities.

Aggregate Workforce Forecast and Its Composition

Table 15.2 brings together the forecasts emerging from individual sectoral studies in Part B and Figure 15.1 provides a graphical illustration. The aggregation process here involved a summation of the central forecast of employment and, where relevant, self-employment for each sector. The resulting forecast of the economy-wide workforce has a variability margin of $\pm300,000$. The latter figure allows for two possibilities: the variability associated with individual sectoral forecasts are not independent of one another; nor are those associated with small and large firms. In both cases, they are offsetting to a certain extent, reflecting the redistributive aspect of job creation in certain sectors or types of firm. This is particularly true with respect to the growth by small firms, much of which is gained at the expense of large firms. It is also worth stressing that in 1985 there were about 200,000 self-employed who were not clearly allocated to any specific industry. As a result, they are not covered in the table for 1985, nor for 1990. Four main points emerge from the results and its associated analysis:

(a)   over the period 1985-90, the size of the employed workforce is expected to show a small decline of about 125,000 - from 23.7 million to 23.58 million. Given that the variability associated with the projected total is $\pm300,000$, the implication is that at the most there could be up to an additional 175,000 jobs by the end of the decade;

(b)   there is, however, expected to be a significant redistribution of jobs in favour of self-employment and services sectors. Self-employment is expected to increase by around 300,000 and marketed services (ie excluding the public sector) by around 600,000. Within services, the main areas of increase will be business services, wholesaling, insurance and finance, leisure and contract cleaning. Within this group, job creation will be concentrated in firms providing business as distinct from household services;

(c)   in every sector, growth in employment is more likely to occur in smaller establishments or firms. Large firms - particularly in energy, manufacturing and construction - are expecting to employ less rather than more;

(d)   the projected shifts towards self-employment and services are expected to be caused by two developments: the continued contraction in the

Table 15.2   Aggregate Forecasts** of Workforce: 1985-90

Sectors:	1985 (thousands)			1990 (thousands)			Average Annual Percentage Change 1985-1990		
	Employment	Self-Employment	Work Force	Employment	Self-Employment	Work** Force	Employment	Self-Employment	Work Force
Primary Industries									
1. Agriculture, Forestry, Fishing	364	291*	655	328	270	598	-2.2	-1.6	-1.9
2. Energy and Water Supply	596	-	596	526	-	526	-2.6	-	-2.6
Manufacturing									
3. Process Industries	779	-	779	728	-	728	-1.5	-	-1.5
4. Engineering and Related Industries	2,549	-	2,549	2,305	-	2,305	-2.2	-	-2.2
5. Light Production Industries	2,042	-	2,042	1,871	-	1,871	-2.0	-	-2.0
Construction									
6. Construction	933	467	1,400	840	510	1,350	-2.2	+2.0	-0.8
Services									
7. Distributive, Financial and Business Services	5,049	1,055*	6,104	5,260	1,225	6,485	+0.9	+3.4	+1.4
8. Transport and Communication	1,266	103	1,369	1,180	113	1,293	-1.5	+2.2	-1.2
9. Leisure and Other Services	2,196	467	2,663	2,397	560	2,957	+2.0	+4.4	+2.4
10. Public Services	5,010	-	5,010	4,950	-	4,950	-0.2	-	-0.2
Total Great Britain	20,784	2,383	23,167	20,385	2,678	23,063	-0.5	+2.7	0.0
Total UK*	21,247	2,461	23,708	20,828	2,753	23,581**	-0.5	+2.6	0.0

* Includes estimates for Northern Ireland.

** Central forecasts with a variability of ±0.3 million

Source: Chapters 4-13

157

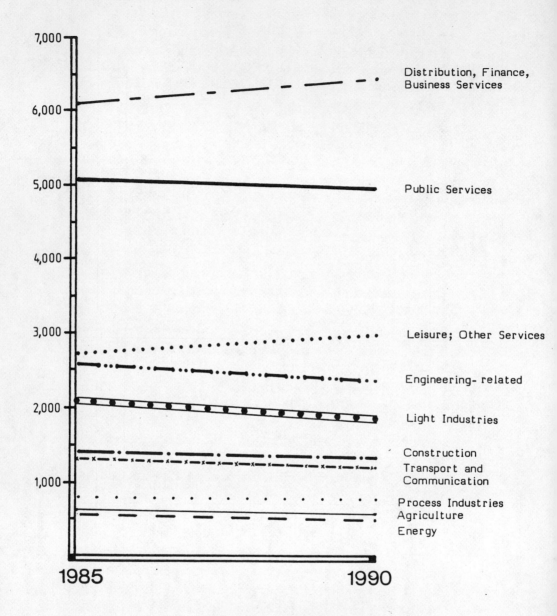

7,000 —

Distribution, Finance, Business Services

6,000 —

5,000 —   Public Services

4,000 —

3,000 —   Leisure; Other Services

                                                Engineering- related

2,000 —   Light Industries

                                                Construction
                                                Transport and
                                                Communication
1,000 —
                                                Process Industries
                                                Agriculture
                                                Energy

1985   1990

Source: Table 15.2

Figure 15.1   Sectoral Change 1985-90

158

workforce of the energy and manufacturing sectors due to uncompetitiveness and the contraction of surplus/uneconomic production capacity, and the resulting adjustments; and the increasing reliance on subcontracting. The latter is expected to favour small firms and self-employed within these sectors providing components, and other sectors providing services. (Table 15.1) Thus the growth in services will be part redistributive and part organic. Of the 600,000 new service jobs (outside the public sector), as an order of magnitude, anything up to 60 per cent is expected to result from redistribution.

Turning to some of the compositional elements, the feasibility study had shown that a majority of organisation could not provide a realistic **numerical** breakdown of their future workforce by various employee categories. Instead, what they could provide was an indication of the direction in which the **proportions** of these categories would move.

Table 15.3 provides an indication of the change in shares of female and part-time (female) employees in each sector's employment over the period 1979-85. It shows that their respective shares increased overall but this was prompted by three service sectors: distributive, financial and business services; leisure and other services, and public services; part-time employees share of jobs being static in all other sectors. As was noted in their respective chapters, employment growth has in these three service sectors particularly favoured part-time employees because of the possibilities of fragmenting and standardising tasks, partly through the use of new technologies, and the need to cover fluctuating work loads. More generally, their recruitment has been favoured by two other factors. First, they are not paid the full set of prevailing fringe benefits on a pro-rata basis; as such their per capita payroll cost is lower for a majority of organisations in the case studies. The reduction in the national insurance rate last year provided an added impetus. Second, because of the flexibility in the hours they choose to work, the part-time staff provide a flexible resource in meeting 'peak hour' demand, particularly in distributive trades, finance, catering and cleaning services. Turning to the future, the evidence emerging from the survey and case studies is given in Table 15.4 and indicates that the share of part-time employees is expected to decline in manufacturing but increase in services, and particularly in large firms. Thus the projected contraction in manufacturing is expected to affect both full- and part-time employees; and the projected expansion in services is expected to favour part-time employees. Overall the share of part-time employees is expected to rise from 21 per cent

Table 15.3   Women and Part-time Staff in Each Sector, 1979-1985

| | Density (Percentage) of: | | | |
| | Female | | Part-time (Female) | |
	1979	1985	1979	1985
Primary Industries				
1. Agriculture, Forestry, Fishing	26	26	9	9
2. Energy and Water Supply	13	14	3	3
Manufacturing				
3. Process Industries	21	19	4	4
4. Engineering and Related Industries	22	21	4	4
5. Light Production Industries	43	42	11	11
Construction				
6. Construction	9	13	4	3
Services				
7. Distributive, Financial and Business Services	50	51	21	24
8. Transport and Communication	19	21	4	4
9. Leisure and Other Services	64	66	37	41
10. Public Services	62	64	30	33
Total Great Britain	42	45	17	21
Total UK*	42	45	17	21

* Includes estimates for Northern Ireland.

Source: Employment Gazette, February 1986

to nearly a quarter of total employment by 1990.

The shares of **temporary or contract** employees are also expected to increase in sectors such as engineering, construction and transport and communication; as employers seek to accomodate longer term fluctuations in their work loads, but not on the same scale as in the case of other employee categories. This observation, however, requires a caveat. The case studies showed that many firms - especially in services - did not distinguish clearly between part-time and temporary employees because the former typically had a high natural wastage rate which many firms built into their planning assumptions.

The implied compositional shifts are indicative of the changes predicted in the industrial structure of the economy. They also reflect the emerging trend towards manning policies that differentiate between the 'core' group and the 'peripheral' group of employees (Atkinson and Meager, 1986). Put simply, the former covers full-time employees with career possibilities; and the latter female, part-time or temporary employees with a high natural wastage rate. Since the last recession, many employers have favoured the recruitment of the latter group in order to achieve flexibility in manpower usage in an uncertain economic environment.

The proportion of **females** in the workforce grew from 42 to 45 per cent between 1979 and 1985, again principally in the service industries but also in construction and the energy sector. (Table 15.3) Over the rest of the decade the proportion of females in employment is expected to increase further on the evidence of the **IMS/OSG Survey** (Table 15.4) and case studies. They may account for nearly half of total employment by 1990. The contributory factors are the growing number of women seeking employment, the expected growth in part-time employment and in service sector employment; both of the last two categories of employment will disproportionately attract females.

Finally, the share of **young employees** is expected to increase in all sectors. This is partly in response to the special policy measures such as the Youth Training Scheme; and partly in response to the new technologies and flexible working methods requiring a more adaptable and trainable workforce.

Comparison With Other Forecasts

Turning now to the final question raised at the beginning of the Chapter; namely, how do the forecasts presented here compare with those emanating from

Table 15.4   Trends in Shares of Employee Categories: 1985-90

(percentages)

	1985-90	
	Will Increase	Will Decrease
(a) Female Employees		
Oil Industries	17	8
Process Industries	19	15
Engineering and Related Industries	25	8
Light Production Industries	32	10
Construction	17	4
Distributive, Financial and Business Services	35	6
Transport and Communication	28	4
Leisure and Other Services	23	5
(b) Part-time Employees		
Oil Industries	5	14
Process Industries	12	19
Engineering and Related Industries	12	20
Light Production Industries	20	21
Construction	7	16
Distributive, Financial and Business Services	30	13
Transport and Communication	24	11
Leisure and Other Services	32	10
(c) Young Employees		
Oil Industries	17	3
Process Industries	32	8
Engineering and Related Industries	43	5
Light Production Industries	41	5
Construction	53	4
Distributive, Financial and Business Services	38	4
Transport and Communication	36	6
Leisure and Other Services	41	8
(d) Temporary & Short-term Employees		
Oil Industries	10	16
Process Industries	23	25
Engineering and Related Industries	26	19
Light Production Industries	19	20
Construction	20	15
Distributive, Financial and Business Services	17	19
Transport and Communication	22	16
Leisure and Other Services	18	17

Source: IMS/OSG Survey

other sources? Currently, there are two forecasting bodies who regularly publish model-based forecasts of employment which draw off historical statistical series and secondary sources - the Centre for Economic Forecasting at the London Business School (LBS), and the Institute of Employment Research (IER) at Warwick University. The Science Policy Research Unit (SPRU) have recently published some one-off forecasts. However, the LBS forecasts are too aggregative and the SPRU forecasts do not follow a set time horizon between industries. A number of other bodies provide forecasts of unemployment but these are not relevant here. As such, the IER is the only organisation to provide detailed sectoral forecasts over the medium term (IER 1985), making them the main reference points for this report.

That said, there still remain definitional differences between the respective forecasts. The IER use the 1968 Standard Industrial Classification; the IMS/OSG study uses the latest (1980) SIC. Thus the respective sectoral groupings are noticeably different. Also, the IER benchmark year is 1984, that for IMS/OSG is 1985. The IER latest forecasts were published in Summer 1985. Bearing these caveats in mind, the respective forecasts for the whole economy are as follows:

| | 1990 | | |
| | Employment | Self-Employment | Total |
	(millions)		
IMS/OSG	20.83	2.75	23.58
IER	21.01	2.70	23.71

Source: IMS/OSG, and IER (1985)

The IMS/OSG employment forecasts are lower by 130,000. This **net difference**, however, obscures pronounced divergences in the sectoral forecasts and the level of detail available about the underlying causes of change. Although the latter cannot be easily compared because of the definitional differences, it is instructive to identify the sectors where the divergences are marked. In this respect, the IMS/OSG employment forecasts are **lower** in agriculture; all manufacturing sectors; transport and communication; and health. In each case, the assessments of the industry-specific circumstances of the organisations participating in this study have led them to put more weight on labour-saving technologies and working methods. In two other areas, the IMS/OSG forecasts are higher: distributive trades and other services. Here, the employers have put more weight on the phenomenon of the subcontracting of the service function than is implicit in the IER projections. The differences at the sectoral level have a major implication. The IMS/OSG forecasts imply a greater shift in the structure of the workforce towards young, female and part-time employees.

More generally, in all cases, there has been more weight put on the post-recessionary developments. The employer-based forecasts of the IMS/OSG study are consistent with the view that these have caused a shift in the employment output relationship on a scale larger than that picked up by econometric models of the UK economy.

Summary

This Chapter has constructed an aggregate forecast of the workforce over the period 1985-90 by bringing together the individual sectoral forecasts developed in Part B. In the process, it has also covered three other aspects: prospective changes in the composition of the workforce; the causal factors, including those that are non-sector specific; and the reasons underlying the differences between the IMS/OSG forecasts and those emanating from other sources.

The aggregation of the sectoral forecasts shows that over the period 1985-90, the employed workforce is expected to decline by about 125,000. This is the net effect of two offsetting changes: a rise of about 300,000 in self-employment and a fall of about 420,000 in employment. Given the error margin of $\pm 300,000$, at most there could therefore be 175,000 additional jobs in the economy by 1990.

In sectoral terms, the biggest employment decline will occur in manufacturing, reflecting continued uncompetitiveness and surplus/uneconomic capacity, and attempts to improve it through reduced employment levels, the introduction of new technologies and improved working methods, and the subcontracting of service functions. Of the 600,000 new jobs expected in the marketed service sectors, (ie excluding public services) up to 60 per cent is likely to involve redistribution between sectors. The rest will constitute organic growth. The potential for further organic job creation in services is, however, seen as limited owing to its lower exposure to foreign trade and the use of new technologies. In most sectors, continuing emphasis on profit maximisation rather than organic growth is seen as a limiting factor on employment growth.

Although the size of the workforce will remain relatively static, the sectoral, status and size composition will shift markedly. Sectors such as agriculture, manufacturing and energy will continue to contract; and those like distribution, finance, business and leisure will continue to expand. These shifts will favour the job prospects of the self-employed, part-time employees, females and the young. They will also favour smaller firms and establishments.

Finally, the IMS/OSG forecast implies a smaller employed workforce compared to the only other published forecast which is based on an econometric model. The IMS/OSG forecast, with special focus on the underlying causes of change, implies greater sectoral redistribution. This is because the employers have put more weight on recent applications of new technologies, labour-saving working methods and subcontracting.

16 Emerging Occupational Trends

Issues

The last Chapter examined the expected trends in the UK workforce and in its compositional elements. The focus is now on the changing occupational structure and the underlying causal factors.

New technologies, changing working methods and the redistribution of jobs between and within sectors are all seen as major determinants of change in the occupational structure, both quantitatively and qualitatively. **Quantitatively,** in the sense that the numbers will increase in certain occupations and decrease in others. **Qualitatively,** in the sense that irrespective of the numerical changes, certain occupations may still become more important in view of either their changing role in the organisation, or the changing content of their work. Also, the skills required within an occupation may change significantly. Since the organisations in the case studies saw both aspects as important, each is covered separately. This Chapter concentrates on the broad quantitative aspect, leaving the qualitative one, relating to skill changes, for the next chapter. Here three questions are considered:

a.   What was the occupational structure in 1985?

b.   What have been the recent trends in the occupational structure and the underlying causes?

c.   How are these trends likely to develop in the medium term to 1990 and what are the underlying causes?

Before answering these questions it is worth emphasising that of all the elements of the workforce, the occupational one is the hardest to quantify. This emerged clearly from the feasibility exercise that preceded this study.

The difficulty arises for four reasons.

First, occupations are traditionally defined in terms of vocational training and/or formal qualifications. But in a large number of organisations in the feasibility study, this criterion did not necessarily reflect the nature of the work that employees undertook. Second, even where the content of work was the main criterion, multi-functions performed under one job introduced notable occupational overlaps to the extent that, in some cases, the same employee could be classified in up to three occupations. Third, for enumeration purposes, organisations often adopted broad groupings that were not very revealing. Typical categories include: direct and indirect employees; or white and blue collar employees, often relating to pay bargaining structures. In so far as such groupings had any occupational dimension, it was usually confined to three broad categories: administrative, technical and clerical; skilled manual; and unskilled manual, together with a functional or divisional breakdown. Rarely did employers collect detailed occupational data for all their workforce. Finally, there were gaps - wide ones, in some cases - between employers' and employees' perceptions of occupations, especially for occupations not requiring further education qualifications.

These factors led to the need for an occupational structure to be devised which had well defined examples in each occupational group so that the respondents were able to construct benchmark estimates for 1985 and indicate the past and likely future changes in them. It was recognised at the outset that while few employers would be able to quantify the magnitude of changes, they would normally be able to show the direction of change across the main groupings and provide insights as to the underlying causes. The analyses from the survey that follow are supplemented with the greater detail emerging from some of the case study organisations who were able to provide more detailed data about expected future trends. Although their experiences can by no means be completely representative, they do illustrate the magnitude and types of changes involved. Two sets of occupational structures were devised, one for production industries and one for service industries. Their compositional elements are described in Appendices A.1 and A.2.

Analytical Framework

In order to facilitate the task of presenting a rather large volume of detailed data, it is useful to develop first a simple analytical framework. Organisations alter their occupational structure because of a number of factors. Of these, the two most important are its volume and method of production.

An increase in the demand for its products or services, for example, can generate an increase in the hiring of employees (e.g. operatives) whose numbers vary directly with the volume of output. As a result of this increase, their percentage in the workforce grows and there is a shift in their favour in the occupational structure. A decrease in demand has a reverse effect. Generally, changes in demand tend to have a disproportionate impact on certain occupations. This kind of effect is called the **demand** effect, hereafter.

A change in the method of working can also have a significant impact. Innovations in the form of new physical technologies and/or work restructuring can favour some occupational groups and disfavour others. For example, the introduction of computers may lead to an increase in the number of hardware and software engineers and a reduction in the number of clerks, some of whose tasks may be automated. Work restructuring that leads to elimination of demarcations may result in jobs that combine or eliminate certain occupations or, at least, reduce their share in workforce. Such physical and organisationally-led changes in the occupational structure of a firm are referred to as the **innovation** effect, hereafter. This has been shown to have one distinct feature: it tends to upgrade certain skills. Sometimes it downgrades others as well, especially where new technologies are involved. The upgrading process usually requires retraining or higher level qualifications.

Over a period of time, therefore, the observed changes in the occupational structure of a firm or the economy are a net outcome of the **demand** effect and the **innovation** effect. Although their relative sizes are difficult to quantify, with the aid of the case studies it is possible to indicate which of the two are more important when analysing the results of the survey.

The earlier analyses of employment change were presented in terms of ten sectors which experienced sector-specific features. A separate Chapter focused on small firms. In occupational terms, however, it proved possible to combine some of these sectors because of common occupational features. Therefore the rest of this Chapter considers occupational changes, first in the **production** industries (energy; process; engineering-related; light production; and construction) and then the **service** industries (distributive, financial and business; transport and communication; leisure; other services; and public services). Reference is made to agriculture in the production industries and also to small firms in all industries.

Production Industries, Occupational Trends and Their Causes to 1990

This section covers the production industries and describes three aspects: the occupational structure as prevailing in 1985; recent trends and their underlying causes; and the expected trends over the rest of this decade and their underlying causes. Each aspect is covered in a separate sub-section.

a.   Occupational Structure in 1985

The occupational structure for all production industries together is indicated in Figure 16.1 and the structures of individual sectors are given in Table 16.1.

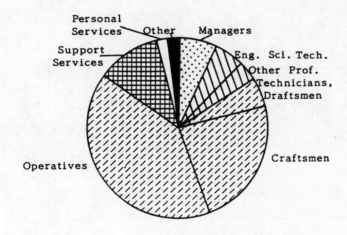

Source: Table 16.1

Figure 16.1   Production Industries: Occupational Structure in 1985

Table 16.1 Production Industries: Occupational Structure in 1985

(percentages)

Occupation:*	Energy	Process Industries	Engineering-Related Industries	Light Production Industries	Construction	Total (Energy, Manufacturing and Construction)
(a) Managers and Administrators	6	6	5	8	9	7
(b) Engineers, Scientists and Technologists	7	8	5	2	10	5
(c) Other Professions	11	4	4	2	3	3
(d) Technicians and Draftsmen	4	5	6	2	7	5
(e) Craftsmen	12	14	26	10	28	19
(f) Operatives	34	47	42	57	31	45
(g) Support Services	18	13	10	15	10	12
(h) Personal Service Occupations	1	2	1	2	1	2
(i) Others	7	1	1	2	1	2
Total (per cent)	100	100	100	100	100	100
Number of Employees Covered	12,283	128,481	335,287	215,344	40,344	731,739
Number of Respondents	29	170	443	407	45	1,094

* See Appendix A.1 for details of occupations in these groups

Source: IMS/OSG Survey

170

For each sector, the structure has been constructed from the data provided by those respondents able to categorise their total workforce in 1985 into the main occupational groups. The last two rows in the table indicate respectively the number of employees and respondent numbers on which the structure is based in each sector. Across all these sectors, a sample of 1,094 employers from all size groups and sectors were able to provide detailed occupational data on their workforce, which when combined totalled over 730,000, over ten per cent of total employment in these sectors. For each sector, the structure has also been corroborated by the detailed figures emerging from the case studies.

The results in Table 16.1 highlight four points. First and foremost, the structures have similarities across the production sectors, especially once allowance is made for the inevitable overlaps between the occupational groups. Second, in each sector operatives constitute the largest group, and the case study firms highlighted how their numbers are most exposed to changes in the volume of production. Third, for all production industries together, up to 60 per cent of the occupations are at the level below craftsman. The proportion varies across the sectors, being as high as 75 per cent in light production industries where, as was observed in Chapter 8, the plant size is usually neither large nor sophisticated; and operations are relatively simple and labour-intensive. Finally, above the level of craftsman, each occupation is relatively small.

b.   Recent Trends and Their Causes

Table 16.2 presents the survey results on trends in the occupational numbers in energy, manufacturing and construction industries over the period 1983-85. It gives the percentage of respondents identifying a given occupation as being 'expanding', or 'contracting'. Under each column heading, it shows the percentage of mentions received by each occupation from the respondents. Thus, one respondent may mention more than one occupation.

Table 16.2   Production Industries: Expanding and Contracting Occupations 1983–85

(Percentages)

Occupation:	Expanding	Contracting
(a) Managers and Administrators	12	7
(b) Engineers, Scientists and Technologists	23	4
(c) Other Professions	5	4
(d) Technicians and Draftsmen	12	5
(e) Craftsmen	14	15
(f) Operatives	17	35
(g) Support Services	15	27
(h) Personal Service Occupations	1	2
(i) Others	1	1
Total (per cent)	100 (N = 1,776)	100 (N = 1,456)

Source: IMS/OSG Survey (see also Appendix C.1)

One occupation has expanded more widely than others: engineers, scientists and technologists (23 per cent). On the other hand, two occupations have been reported as having contracted more widely than others: operatives (35 per cent) and support services (27 per cent). The last of these covers mainly clerical and sales employees. As a broad generalisation, the contraction is more evident in occupations that are less skill-intensive. When the incidence of expansion and contraction are considered together they indicate a shift in favour of occupations that have a higher skill or knowledge content. This picture at the aggregate level is corroborated by the experiences of the individual sectors (Appendix C.1).

The shift, however, masks the differential role of the demand effect and the innovation effect. The case studies shed light on these. First, the demand effect has been negative amongst most of the medium and larger employers - namely those with a headcount in excess of 200 in the period 1983-85. They continued to reduce their numbers in part as a lagged response to the 1979-81 recession, in order to bring manning levels closer to output needs, thereby improving productivity. This negative demand effect was reinforced by the innovation effect because these employers were also introducing new technologies and labour saving working methods. In the case of agriculture, forestry and fishing, the innovation effect has been strong and acted independently of the demand effect.

Singly or in combination, the two effects reduced the numbers in all the occupations at the level of craftsman and below. For example, one water pump manufacturer not only closed two factories but also introduced a Computer Aided Design and Manufacturing (CAD-CAM) system at its main plant. The former led to redundancies of operatives and clerical employees. The latter caused redundancies of junior draftsmen but upgrading of the skills of the craftsmen, who now collaborate with senior product designers and tool room engineers, as well as being responsible for the programming, setting and low level repair and maintenance of the Computer Numerically Controlled (CNC) machines. The total job losses accounted for 15 per cent of the workforce. The complex relationship between the demand and innovation effects is further illustrated by the food division of a major national company which closed one uneconomic factory with out-dated technology and a poor product, shedding 700 jobs, the majority of them unskilled operatives. In the same year, it opened a new factory producing a higher volume of a more successful product using the latest technology, but requiring only 100 staff, the majority of whom were skilled.

Second, in contrast, many smaller employers (employing under 200 people) have experienced a positive demand effect. Their volume of output has increased leading to increases particularly in occupations at craft level and below.

Their numbers in occupations above the craft level do not appear to have been expanded so noticeably. These smaller companies have not experienced a strong **innovation** effect on anything like the scale of their larger counterparts. This was partly because their adoption of new technologies has been slow, if not negligible; and partly because they see their scope for further work restructuring being limited, given their prevailing functional flexibility, facilitated by having a small labour force. Apart from these reasons, in the case of very small firms (covered in Chapter 14), the higher level occupations are filled by proprietors and their family members and are relatively stable in number. For example, a small clothing manufacturer experienced an exceptional increase in demand on account of the closure of large competitors in the area. It bought one of the closed factories and hired 50 extra machinists, equivalent to a third of its original labour force. The machines came with the factory. They were old, not microprocessor-based as are the modern versions. Key functions such as production planning, marketing, accounts and recruitment continued to be performed by the proprietor and his existing management team, consisting mainly of family members.

Thus in the recent past, employers in the production industries have been changing their occupational structure, increasing the human capital component through a combination of a negative demand effect and the innovation effect. While the demand effect has been positive in smaller employers and favoured less skill-intensive occupations, it has not been enough to counter the reductions by the larger companies.

c.   Future Trends and Their Causes

The past trends towards higher skill levels are expected to continue over the period to 1990. Table 16.3 gives the occupational changes expected by the employers in the survey. Under each figure the brackets indicate whether the response has been dominated by smaller, medium, large or all employers. When the 'increases' and 'decreases' are considered together, it emerges that employment in four occupations is expected to increase. They are: engineers, scientists and technologists; other professions; technicians and draftsmen; and craftsmen.

The 'increases' in the first two include a significant representation of large and medium sized firms. The 'decreases' are notably high for all occupations at the level of craftsman and below; and in each case the response is dominated by large employers (employing in excess of 500). In fact, large

174

Table 16.3   Production Industries: Occupational Changes in Period 1985-90*

(percentages)

Occupation:	Likely To:		
	Increase	Remain Static	Decrease
(a) Managers and Administrators	25 (All)	60 (All)	15 (Large)
(b) Engineers, Scientists, Technologists	55 (All)	41 (All)	4 (Large)
(c) Other Professions	22 (All)	71 (All)	7 (Large)
(d) Technicians and Draftsmen	44 (Medium)	47 (All)	9 (Large)
(e) Craftsmen	36 (Small/Medium)	44 (All)	20 (Large)
(f) Operatives	41 (Small)	26 (All)	33 (All)
(g) Support Services	27 (Small)	47 (Medium)	26 (Large)
(h) Personal Service Occupations	10 (Small)	73 (All)	(17) (Large)
(i) Others	32 (Small)	50 (All)	18 (Large)

*   Under each percentage is given the type of employers dominating the result. Four employer-types have been designated for this purpose: **Large** (over 500); **Medium** (200-499); **Small** (under 200); **All** (no dominance by size)

Source: IMS/OSG Survey

175

employers dominate all 'decreases' reported in the survey and the case studies. The occupations they expect to increase are the managers; engineers, scientists and technologists; and other professions. This is indicative of the continuation of the negative demand effect and the innovation effect, as uneconomic capacity is reduced and the companies seek to increase competitiveness through the introduction of new technologies and improved working methods. In the case of agriculture, forestry and fishing, the innovation effect will continue to operate independently of the demand effect and follow the long-term trend. Thus, the prospective reduction in employment discussed in the last chapter will impinge most on the less skill-intensive occupations.

On the other hand, the demand effect will continue to be positive in smaller (under 200 staff) firms. As their employment grows they will increase their intake of all occupations, **including** the less skill-intensive ones. As shown in Chapter 14, in established small firms employment growth over the rest of this decade is also likely to favour occupations at the level of operative and below.

Once again, these are generalisations applying across the production industries. Results for the individual sectors are given in Appendix C.2-C.6. Although there are some inter-sectoral variabilities they do not detract from the substantive point that the employers surveyed and interviewed expect the occupational structure over the rest of the decade to favour the more skill-intensive occupations. Equally, they highlight the importance of smaller employers in creating job opportunities in less skill-intensive occupations.

Three contrasting examples from the case studies serve to illustrate these points - one covering an oil company, another a growing, smaller food manufacturer, and a third a manufacturing company. The oil company has extensive engineering and chemical operations because of its involvement in the North Sea and 'downstream' refining. Currently its total UK employment is 5,000. By 1990, this will be reduced by at least 10 per cent. The projected occupational shifts given in Table 16.4 are due to four factors.

First, in the current round of developments in the North Sea it is relying on recovery techniques that are more technology-intensive than the conventional platforms, thus increasing the company's dependence on highly qualified engineering and electronics based manpower, and associated professional manpower. Second, the drive towards complete functional flexibility at the technician level and below will reduce the number of operatives on the oil platforms. Third, the planned enhancement of computer capability at the on-shore supply bases will reduce the number of clerical support and draftsmen. Finally, the current restructuring of the refinery capacity will reduce the number of transport workers (classified here as operatives).

Table 16.4   Occupational Changes in an Oil Company: 1985-1990

Occupation:	Numbers		Percentage Change 1985-1990
	1985	1990	
(a) Managers and Administrators	50	50	0
(b) Engineers, Scientists etc	500	585	17
(c) Other Professions	400	450	13
(d) Technicians and Draftsmen	100	90	-10
(e) Craftsmen	1,400	1,440	3
(f) Operatives	1,000	720	-28
(g) Support Services (clerical)	1,300	945	-28
(h) Personal Service Occupations	150	135	-10
(i) Others	100	85	-15
Total Employment	5,000	4,500	-10

Source: IMS/OSG Case Study

In the case of the small food manufacturer, its employment is expected to double over the rest of this decade, from the 1985 level of 150. With one of its very large competitors ceasing trading, this manufacturer has become the main supplier to two national chains of food retailers. As a result, it is expanding its present factory and will take on mainly machinists, packers and transport workers. Its occupational structure is expected to change as shown in Table 16.5. The change will be mainly demand-led and the expansion will mainly benefit the operatives.

A final example is of a multi-sectoral manufacturing company expecting significant output growth which it expects to achieve with improved working methods, increasing use of new technologies, and 'working smarter'. As a result its overall employment is planned to fall by ten per cent; the main reduction affecting operatives, clerical and other support staff, while the number of professional staff will grow in commercial areas and marketing (Table 16.6).

Table 16.5   Occupational Changes in a Food Manufacturer: 1985-1990

Occupation:	Numbers		Percentage Change 1985-1990
	1985	1990	
(a) Managers and Administrators	4	6	50
(b) Engineers, Scientists etc	2	3	50
(c) Other Professions	1	2	50
(d) Technicians and Draftsmen	9	18	50
(e) Craftsmen	15	24	60
(f) Operatives	90	210	133
(g) Support Services	15	21	40
(h) Personal Service Occupations	7	6	-15
(i) Others	8	10	25
Total Employment	150	300	100

Source: IMS/OSG Case Study

Table 16.6   Occupational Changes in a Manufacturing Company: 1985-90

Occupation:	Numbers		Percentage Change 1985-90
	1985	1990	
a) Managers	64	60	-6
b) Engineers, Scientists etc	160	165	+3
c) Other Professionals	95	105	+11
d) Technicians	184	175	-5
e) Craftsmen	412	380	-8
f) Operatives	794	695	-12
g) Support Services (Clerical)	240	180	-25
h) Personal Services	95	80	-16
Total Employment	2044	1840	-10

Source: IMS/OSG Case Study

Service Industries, Occupational Trends and Their Causes to 1990

Following the pattern in the previous section, three aspects are covered for the service industries: occupational structure as prevailing in 1985; the factors underlying the change in the recent past; and expected changes over the rest of the decade, along with causal factors.

a. Occupational Structure in 1985

Table 16.7 gives the structure for each of the service sectors (excluding public services) based on the data from a sample of 861 organisaions from all size groups and sectors, who between them employed 825,000 people; equal to ten per cent of total employment in these sectors. Figure 16.2 presents an overview of the structure in all the marketed sectors. They have only one common feature: the relatively low proportions in the managerial and professional groups. Beyond that, there are notable differences, reflecting the differences in the nature of activities.

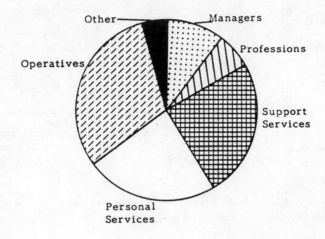

Source: Table 16.7

Figure 16.2   Service Industries: Occupational Structure in 1985

In the distributive, financial and business services sector, the support services group predominates and principally involves sales assistants and clerical employees. In the leisure sector, the personal services group dominates, involving waiters, bar staff, cooks, cleaners and porters. In transport and communication, the operatives, technicians, and craftsmen group predominates, as it does in 'other services' which covers the varied activities such as research and development; contract cleaning; laundry and dry cleaning; and hairdressing, where, there are large numbers of low skilled operatives. In each of the sectors the predominance reflects the basic nature of their respective activities.

Table 16.7   Service Industries: Occupational Structure in 1985

(percentages)

Occupation:*	Distributive, Financial and Business Services	Transport and Communication	Leisure Services	Other Services	All Marketed Services
(a) Managers and Administrators	10	7	10	6	9
(b) All Professions	10	7	3	4	7
(c) Support Services (Clerical and Sales)	42	19	3	12	25
(d) Personal Services	17	7	75	10	23
(e) Technicians, Craftsmen and Operatives	12	58	8	65	32
(f) Others	9	2	1	3	4
Total (per cent)	100	100	100	100	100
Number of Employees Covered	349,114	271,900	134,986	69,204	825,204
Number of Respondents	560	104	115	82	861

* See Appendix A.2 for details of occupations in these groups

Source: IMS/OSG Survey

b.   Recent Trends and Their Causes

Table 16.8 gives the survey results on recent trends in the size of the occupations in services (excluding public services). It gives the percentage of mentions received by each occupation under the two headings: 'expanding' or 'contracting'. It is clear that the expansion has been widely based and particularly benefited four occupations: support services, especially sales (31 per cent); professions (28 per cent); operatives, technicians, and craftsmen (17 per cent); and managers (17 per cent). Occupationally, the contraction is narrowly based; being more evident in support services, especially clerical and related (45 per cent) and operatives, technicians, and

180

Table 16.8   Services*:   Expanding, and Contracting Occupations,
              1983-85

(percentages)

Occupation:	Expanding	Contracting
(a) Managers and Administrators	17	11
(b) All Professions	28	10
(c) Support Services	31	45
(d) Personal Service Occupations	6	4
(e) Operatives, Technicians and Draftsmen	17	29
(f) Others	2	1
Total	100	100
	(N = 955)	(N = 637)

*   excluding public services

Source: IMS/OSG Survey (see also Appendix C.7)

craftsmen (29 per cent).

According to the case studies, the expansion has been underpinned substantially by a positive demand effect in every employer category. As seen in Chapters 10 and 12, there has been an overall increase in employment in distributive, financial and business services, and leisure and other services, particularly favouring part-time work. To a lesser extent, the innovation effect, too, has been at work. This has come in the form of new technologies and more centralised organisational structures in five main employing industries: distribution, finance, transport, communication and leisure. Under it, services have been increasingly automated affecting/reducing the need for clerical and administrative occupations in particular. Elsewhere the increased reliability of vehicles and other equipment has not only reduced service intervals but it has also reduced the need for maintenance staff, especially in transport, communication and repair services.

As Appendix C.7 shows, there is some inter-sectoral variability. But on the whole the positive demand effect has predominated and helped increased employment in two occupational groups: support services and personal services. To a certain extent, this tendency has been reinforced by the innovation effect in so far as new technologies have permitted standardisation, fragmentation and automatic supervision of work, thereby facilitating the growth in part-time jobs in these two occupational groups. In all, the service industries' occupational structure has shifted towards less skill-intensive occupations such as cashiers in banks, sales assistants in retailing and cleaners in other services. One example illustrates the point. In one fast growing clearing bank, the introduction of the 'front office' counter terminals led to the automation of the book-keeping aspects of the cashier function. As a result, the bank increased its number of part-time cashiers by 30 per cent. Without computerisation, the volume of throughput they now handle would have required 20 per cent extra full-time cashiers. This process led to a growth in staff numbers higher than would have been the case if full-time cashiers had been recruited instead. Thus computerisation facilitated the employment of part-time cashiers and business growth promoted an increase in their numbers.

When examining the future trends, the analysis of the past prompts an important observation. The new jobs created in the service industries have been mainly in low skill-intensive occupations - that is occupations that do not necessarily involve formal education qualifications, a pre-defined period of apprenticeship, or standards-based training.

c.   Future Trends and Their Causes

The employers expect that the above underlying factors, particularly the demand effect, will continue to operate. Table 16.9 shows the expectations of 'increases' and 'decreases' for each occupation over the period to 1990. The main feature of the results is that the 'increases' far outweigh the 'decreases' for every occupation. There are, however, differences between sectors and sizes of firms (Appendix C.8-C.10). The expectation of increases in distributive, financial and business services is primarily a reflection of the continuing positive demand effect, which is expected to affect organisations in all size groups. In transport and communication, and leisure and other services by contrast, a notable feature is the dominance of large employers in the 'decreases' proportions. Although such proportions are small, they reflect the continuing innovation effect. According to the case studies, there is likely to be further capacity rationalisation in the leisure and transport and communication industries, as well as in retail, wholesale and banking, particularly by the larger employers. This is expected to involve the closure of smaller units and the expansion of the larger ones, and the more intensive use of new technologies; all involving reductions in every occupation. However, their combined effect is not expected to be as large as the strong demand effect expected by small and medium size employers, with the result that growth will continue to favour the low skill-intensive occupations.

The expected changes described above are illustrated by a retail group, which developed a profile of its occupational changes over the period 1985-90 when its total headcount is expected to increase by 10 per cent. This is given in Table 16.10. Here the demand effect is likely to benefit the three low skill-intensive groups: support services, mainly part-time sales staff; personal services, such as catering; and craftsmen and operatives involving specific occupations such as butchers, bakers and lorry drivers. It will also benefit the professional occupations such as accountancy, marketing and buying as the head office functions are expanded. On the other hand, unskilled occupations which have involved casual workers in all areas are likely to contract because their work is expected to be performed as a subsidiary activity by other occupational groups. Overall, however, the projected occupational changes in this service firm provide an interesting contrast with those for the oil company exposed to the innovation effect, benefiting mainly high skill-intensive occupations (Table 16.4).

Table 16.9   Service Industries: Occupational Changes in Period 1985-90*

(percentage)

		Likely To:		
		Increase	Remain Static	Decrease
(a)	Managers and Administrators	39 (Small)	54 (Small/Medium)	7 (All)
(b)	All Professions	47 (Small/Medium)	48 (All)	5 (Large)
(c)	Support Services	45 (Small/Medium)	39 (Small/Medium)	16 (Large)
(d)	Personal Services	28 (Small/Medium)	63 (All)	9 (Large)
(e)	Technicians, Craftsmen and Operatives	48 (All)	39 (All)	13 (All)
(f)	Others	43 (Small/Medium)	42 (All)	15 (Large)

* Under each percentage is given the type of employers dominating the
result. Four employer-types have been designated for this purpose: Large,
(over 500); Medium, (200-499); Small, (under 200); All, (no dominance by
size)

Source: IMS/OSG Survey

Table 16.10   Occupational Changes in a Retail Firm: 1985-90

Occupation		Numbers		Percentage Change 1985-90
		1985	1990	
(a)	Managers and Administrators	4,250	3,850	-10
(b)	All Professions	1,500	1,925	28
(c)	Support Services	14,000	15,950	14
(d)	Personal Service Occupations	3,000	3,575	19
(e)	Operatives, Technicians and Craftsmen	1,250	1,650	32
(f)	Others	1,000	550	-45
	Total Employment	25,000	27,500	10

Source: IMS/OSG Case Study

The Public Sector, Occupational Trends and Their Causes to 1990

In the public sector, the changing occupational balance will largely reflect the changing **demand** effect, in this case service provision. However within certain occupational groups - particularly in administration and clerical activities - changing work methods and the increasing application of office technologies have been having a significant **innovation** effect in the recent past.

In the public sector there are two dominant, largely sector-specific occupations: teaching, involving over 500,000 people; and medical, nursing and welfare occupations, involving in the former two cases over 500,000 people (inlcuding unqualified staff) in the health service, and a further 200,000 staff in local authorities. In the case of teachers a continuing reduction in the pupil population over the period to 1990, allied to continuing financial restraint, will mean that the number of teachers will continue to fall, possibly by up to one per cent per annum. Much will depend on the rate of school closures. However, there is expected to be a growth in personal service occupations involving part-time jobs in supervising school lunch breaks resulting from changes to teachers' contracts. In the case of medical and nursing staff a continued increase in numbers is expected as more resources are devoted to direct patient care. The number of social welfare staff, particularly semi-skilled welfare helpers and home helps, is also expected to expand in response to the growing demand for social services from an aging population. The magnitude of change in the number of jobs in these latter two groups is hard to quantify becuase of the large numbers of part-time staff involved and the ease with which different authorities can alter the balance of full and part-time staff within a total budget, to adjust staffing levels to service needs and staff availability. Another smaller occupational group that is planned to expand relates to the police and prison service, together with the courts and probation service. Across these groups, numbers total over 150,000 and are expected to continue to rise over the period to 1990.

More generally across the public sector the numbers of all other categories of staff are expected to fall, particularly the administrative and clerical staff, due to a combination of changing service provision, financial restraint, improved working methods and the use of new technologies. The number of largely unskilled support staff in areas such as catering, maintenance and cleaning is also expected to show a marked reduction due to a mixture of new working methods, and the contracting out of activities, although the latter will benefit other service sectors.

The changing balance between occupational groups and shift towards professional and skilled groups is shown by a case study based on the details from one Health Region whose resources are growing and is expecting to increase its overall employment over the period to 1990. This is well above the national average (Table 16.11). The benefit of growth accrues to the medical, nursing and professional groups.

Table 16.11   Occupational Changes in a Health Authority: 1985-90

Occupation:	Numbers		Percentage Change 1985-90
	1985	1990	
Medical/Dental	2,100	2,250	7
Nursing	21,500	22,700	6
Other Nursing Professions	1,725	2,000	16
Scientific and Technical	2,000	2,170	8
Admin/Clerical	5,500	5,525	0.4
Ambulance	940	940	0
Works	1,500	1,515	1
Ancilliary	7,950	7,625	-4
Total	43,215	44,725	3

Source: IMS/OSG Case Study

Summary

This Chapter has set out the main occupational charcteristics of employment in 1985 and the expected pattern of changes over the period to 1990 and their underlying causes. The main finding is that the production industries have broadly similar occupational structures while the service industries display notable inter-sectoral differences in their structures, reflecting the differences in their activities. In all sectors, the occupational structures have been changing and are expected to continue to do so over the rest of this decade.

In the **production industries**, the occupational structure is changing as the knowledge content and skill intensity of work have been increasing. It will continue to do so with expected increase in the employment of engineers, scientists, technologists, multiple-skilled craftsment in response to the continuing applications of new technologies and better working methods. Also, employers have been reducing their employment in occupations at the level of craftsman and below to eliminate surplus manning and increase productivity through improved working methods and the introducion of new technologies. This trend is expected to continue over the rest of this decade.

Within this general picture there are significant exceptions. Smaller firms have recruited, and are likely to continue to increase their employment, in the occupations at the level of craftsman and below due to growth in their business volume. On the whole, such firms regard themselves as relatively less technologically innovative, but more flexible in their response to the market and in their use of their manpower resources.

In the **service industries**, the occupational structure is likely to shift in favour of less skill-intensive personal and support services occupations. The number of full-time employees in such occupations is likely to decline, mainly amongst larger employers, in response to new technologies and organisational changes. However, these changes are also expected to promote part-time opportunities on a significant scale in these occupations. The growing sophistication of operations is also likely to promote opportunities for professional occupations. In the public sector the numbers of medical, nursing, and welfare staff will grow, as will those in the police, prison service and courts. The numbers in teaching will continue to fall as will those in all other areas of the public service, especially among the less skilled occupations.

Figure 16.3 below summarises the expected occupational trends in the production and service groups of industries over the period to 1990.

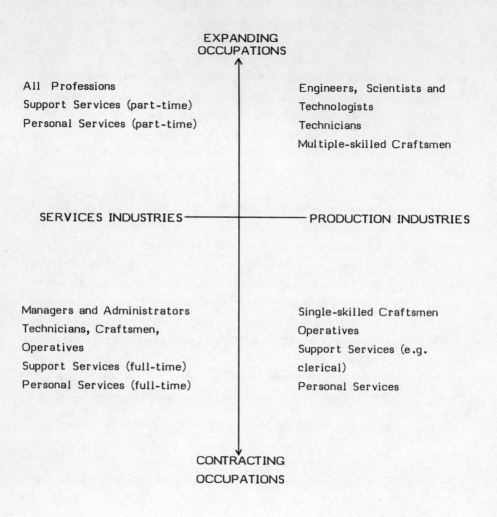

EXPANDING
OCCUPATIONS

All Professions
Support Services (part-time)
Personal Services (part-time)

Engineers, Scientists and
Technologists
Technicians
Multiple-skilled Craftsmen

SERVICES INDUSTRIES —————————— PRODUCTION INDUSTRIES

Managers and Administrators
Technicians, Craftsmen,
Operatives
Support Services (full-time)
Personal Services (full-time)

Single-skilled Craftsmen
Operatives
Support Services (e.g.
clerical)
Personal Services

CONTRACTING
OCCUPATIONS

Figure 16.3   The Changing Balance of Occupations

Source: IMS/OSG Study

17 Key Occupations and Skills

Introduction

The objective of this study has been to identify the changing balance of occupations and employment over the period to 1990, and the underlying causes. The previous chapters have developed the broad perspective. However, the emerging picture is only partial because it still needs to be complemented by an analysis of the important qualitative trends emerging in key occupations. For example, some occupations may increase in importance within the organisation as a result of changes in their skill content or because their role in the organisation changes. Such factors need not be accompanied by numerical growth. They may, however, require increased attention in respect of the training and development of the people in, or about to enter, these occupations.

By their very nature, such qualitative changes are not easy to ascertain directly. However, the survey was able to elicit data on those occupations that employers regarded as 'most vital to the organisation's future business performance'. It was also able to identify those that had presented them with 'recruitment difficulties' in 1985. This gave a barometer of the relative availability of these skills in the labour market at that time. Recourse to the case studies provides an understanding of why these occupations were perceived as vital and what were their most important characteristics, independently of an increase in their numbers. The reasons were normally related to changing organisational needs and focused on one or more of four factors: expansion in the skill requirements of work due to rising performance standards; increase in the knowledge content of work requiring higher educational qualifications; innate attributes in areas such as sales and marketing; and work experience underpinned by growing familarity of the organisations' products and customers.

This Chapter seeks to develop them in detail, with reference to four occupational groups perceived as vital: **managers, engineers, scientists and technologists; other professions;** and an amalgam of **other** occupational groups (these are defined in the survey, see Appendix A.1, A.2)

Managers

One clear overriding message came out from the survey and the case-study interviews: that managers were seen as the key source of most organisations' future success. This applied across all sectors and sizes of organisation, in both the private and the public sector. The survey shows that in 1985 managers (and administrators) accounted for about seven per cent of employment in the production industries and nine per cent in the services sector. While the numbers varied between individual sectors, partly reflecting the size distribution of organisations in the sector, they were not a numerically large occupational group within the total labour force. Nor were their numbers expected to change markedly over the period to 1990, as the growth in their numbers in small organisations was expected to be countered by a reduction in many of the larger organisations as they continue to improve organisational structures and reduce layers of management.

The survey identified the occupations perceived as 'vital' for future business performance over the rest of this decade. In production as well as service sectors, the managerial group received the highest mentions: 25 per cent and 35 per cent respectively (Tables 17.1 and 17.2). These percentages were also high among the vacancies that were 'Hard to Fill' in 1985 (see Appendices C.1 and C.7).

The role of the manager is seen to be changing in terms of both work content and the need for higher standards of performance. In many case studies, it was emphasised that both work content and improved performance will increasingly require four kinds of skills: planning skills to cope with the strategic element of their work; commercial skills to allocate and prioritise resources within the plan; human relations skills to secure the plan's acceptance; and administrative skills to implement it. A large footwear firm illustrated the point. In it, the managerial function had three elements: strategic, tactical and operational. As the names imply, the first involved devising strategic corporate plans; the second involved choice of methods in translating them into action; and the third involved day-to-day administration. Prior to the recession, the last element had predominated. Since then, the balance had

Table 17.1 Production Industries: Occupations Perceived as Vital for Business Performance:1985-89

Vital Occupation:	Energy %	Processing %	Engineering %	Consumer %	Construction %	Manufacturing Total %
Managers and Administrators	21	26	23	28	31	25
Engineers, Scientists and Technologists	36	27	29	15	14	23
Other Professions	5	2	2	4	9	3
Technicians and Draftsmen	5	11	13	10	4	11
Craftsmen	7	12	12	12	26	12
Operatives	7	8	8	12	9	9
Support Services	18	13	11	16	5	13
Personal Service Occupations	-	1	1	1	1	1
Others	-	-	3	2	-	2
	100	100	100	100	100	100
	(N = 56)	(N = 396)	(N = 1,068)	(N= 973)	(N = 97)	(N = 2,590)

Source: IMS/OSG Survey

191

Table 17.2   Services: Occupations Perceived as Vital for
Business Performance 1985-89

Vital Occupation:	Retailing	Transport & Communication	Leisure	'Other' Services	Services Total
Managers and Administrators	33	38	44	33	35
Other Professions	23	10	7	22	19
Technicians and Draftsmen	10	13	8	22	11
Support Services	30	32	18	19	28
Personal Service Occupations	3	4	22	2	6
Others	1	3	1	3	1
	100	100	100	100	100
	(N =1,000)	(N = 188)	(N = 214)	(N = 146)	(N = 1,548)

Source: IMS/OSG Survey

tilted the other way, causing a cultural shock for its older managers while the firm has had difficulty recruiting managers with qualifications and proven track records in planning and implementation of corporate plans.

However, even where planning is not essential, it was clear that the content of work is expanding, as in a construction company where managers are now expected to have keyboard, diagnostic and analytical skills to use the on-line computer facility and analyse the data in their day-to-day functions. The task of data access and analysis was previously done by qualified support staff and a consequence of managers broadening their skills was that a layer of staff support had been removed. In a food manufacturing firm, factory managers are being increasingly involved in sales and marketing by delegating the day-to-day administrative tasks to their subordinates. In a tobacco firm, the sales force had been run down because managers are now handling sales through the value added networks which gives them computerised access to their retailers and wholesalers. In an engineering firm, the product portfolio has been enhanced to cover the 'know-how'. The sales managers are now expected to acquire a familiarity of both the technical details of the new service and special skills in selling non-tangible products.

The case studies also showed that many of the larger firms in the production industries are decentralising their operations, reducing the size of their head offices and the numbers of specialist and support staff. The corollary is the increasing accountability of local managements. However, the amount of specialist support available to support the units is being reduced so the managers are having to broaden their skill base and use more discretion while at the same time working to more specific performance related objectives. Salary systems are also often being adjusted to reflect this greater recognition of performance.

In the service sector where large chains of outlets prevail, as in retailing and financial services, the role of local managers is also undergoing a change. For example, in retailing the function of managing the stores is changing dramatically. It is becoming both more varied and specialised, requiring four kinds of skills: planning, knowledge-based, social, and human relations. Between them, they are meant to promote professionalism on the one hand and entrepreneurship on the other. Planning involves anticipating and catering for changing consumer tastes. Knowledge pertains to products and consumer psychology. Social skills are a pre-requisite for inter-personal communication and customer counselling; as are human relations skills for effective staff management. Managers are viewed here as an increasingly vital resource because they co-ordinate all activity of outlets that are radically different from those of the last decade. One retail group found that a 'good' manager in a clothing shop could boost sales by 20 per cent compared to a less able manager in the similar circumstances. The managerial function in head offices is also seen to be changing with the demarcations between managers and professionals being weakened through two avenues. First, management trainees are acquiring qualifications and skills in disciplines such as marketing, operational research, economics and computing. Second, the specialist functions are operating on a team basis, involving both managers and professionals; the object being to encourage interchange of experience and knowledge.

In the public sector, functional specialists have in the past dominated the management of their functions. Now two developments are under way: an increase in the management skills of those in management roles; and enhancement of the role of the 'professional manager', as administrators become managers with greater responsibilities for decision making. This is most visibly highlighted in the National Health Service where a new management structure has been developed under which managers span a complete unit such as a hospital or a district, rather than a function such as nursing or administrative groups as in the past. This is being achieved both by the recruitment of generalist managers from outside the Health Service and by developing and training staff from within. Finally, in small firms, the manager, being in effect the first member of staff, is clearly seen to have a key role in developing the firm through a broad base of skills.

To summarise, although neither numerically large nor significantly growing, the managerial group is seen by employers in all sectors and sizes of firms as being the most vital occupation for their future success. Its work content is changing, requiring both a higher level of performance and a broader base of skills.

Engineers, Scientists and Technologists

This was the second vital group within the production industries (Table 17.1). Numerically it is not large, accounting for about five per cent of those in the production industries and considerably fewer in the service sector in 1985. A wide range of disciplines is included under this generic title: from biologists working in the pure sciences, to electronics engineers and metallurgists, and to civil engineers. Such staff are normally graduates. As shown in the last Chapter, this occupation has been showing signs of most rapid expansion in recent and future years (Table 16.3). It is also the one for which employers in the production industries had the greatest recruitment difficulties in 1985 (Appendix C.7). Within the production industries, engineers, scientists and technologists were concentrated in the energy, process, and engineering and related industries where they were perceived to be of greatest importance to companies' future success. The clear message drawing these occupations together across all sectors is the need for microelectronics and information technology (IT) skills - either in terms of technical specialists such as electronics and software engineers; or in other occupations, such as production engineers, needing the skills to apply the technology to the development and integration of new manufacturing systems, or architects using Computer Aided Design (CAD) techniques, or chemists using computers for monitoring and analyses processes.

The current and likely future shortage of these skills has recently been documented; as have the factors determining their growth in numbers in the IT producer and user industries across all sectors of the economy. The need for professional IT staff could rise by 25 per cent and total 250,000 by 1990 (Connor, Pearson, 1986). The IMS/OSG survey and the case studies highlighted the importance of these skills within the context of the organisation's overall employment structure - both in the electronics industry to develop the technology, and in the rest of the production and service industries to increasingly apply IT to production areas and services. The latter highlights the need for multi-skilled personnel who could, for example, combine production and electronics skills; or design using IT in the form of computer aided design. Increasingly, these technical specialists are working in teams, and there is a growing need for them to have project management and commercial skills. A particular example of the latter was highlighted in the electronics sector where contractors in the defence and telecoms areas are having to move from a cost plus pricing structure to competitive tendering. As well as increasing the need for commercial awareness within the technical project team, this is also extending technical staff's involvement in customer liaison and marketing. Another growing need is for staff with experience of specific applications of IT; for example to help in the development and application of a financial management system or an information network.

Other constituent occupations seen as becoming increasingly important over the period to 1990 are production and manufacturing engineers, particularly those who can work in terms of 'systems' embracing for example, design, materials handling and manufacturing; and who can use new technologies to boost productivity, improve product reliability and increase flexibility of production. Design skills to increase the competitiveness of products were also highlighted as being in growing demand, as are the new skills related to biotechnology; although the latter will only involve very small numbers of people, mainly in the pharmaceutical, food and drink industries. Technical sales staff are another important group, especially in relation to electronics based products. The growing need for skills relating to project and staff management and commercial awareness was highlighted across all disciplines.

The importance of these occupations is underpinned by increasing knowledge content - acquired through higher education - of products and processes; as well as the trend towards team work involving non-specialists.

Other Professions

This diverse group, ranging from accountants to training officers (see Appendix A.1 and A.2), was highlighted by many employers, particularly in the service sector, as being vital. The numbers involved are again small. The specific occupations causing most concern were **data processing** staff where there were national shortages affecting all sectors. The companies expect growth in this category to continue to the end of the decade in line with expansion in the use of IT and alongside the growing demand for electronics and software engineers noted above. In many companies the role of central data processing (DP) staff is changing as they need to move away from being 'back room' specialists to directly help the user choose and apply the new technologies. This is requiring many DP staff to acquire interpersonal and advisory skills and to develop a better appreciation of the needs of individual users. This is further blurring functional boundaries.

A second 'vital' occupation identified in this group was **accountants**, where again the numbers being employed are expected to continue to grow. Many employers have also been experiencing recruitment difficulties. The need for improved and extended financial management systems, and linking branch networks in the service sectors, for example, is a driving force for growth. The growing trend to more autonomous operating units as a result of decentralisation is also generating the demand for more management staff to have financial skills, and is often leading to the appointment of a financial specialist in each unit. The use of information technology was again a growing component of the work.

Marketing and **professional sales** staff are another key resource where there was a common wish to improve the quality and effectiveness of staff; and recruitment difficulties were regularly reported as companies sought 'good' experienced staff.

In the health and welfare services there is expected to be a continued growth in the demand for professional **medical, nursing** and **welfare staff** in line with the expansion in services, in the case of nurses some recruitment difficulties are being experienced.

In all cases, however, the importance of this occupational group is underpinned by the need for higher education-based knowledge and skills to work across a number of specialist disciplines as products and/or production methods or services became increasingly based on science and technology.

Other Occupations

For a number of organisations, **technicians and craftsmen** were reported as being key for their future success. The growth in numbers involved is again relatively small compared to other occupations. But this does not detract from the growing need for skills enhancement in these occupations. The case studies showed that both technological factors and weakening job demarcations are promoting the importance of multiple-skilled craftsmen with mechanical, electrical, electronic and hydraulic based skills. For example, one case study firm making brake-pads for vehicles upgraded the entire plant integrating twelve previous stages of production into three. All the craft occupations, formerly split into three distinct groups, are now combined into a general purpose occupation that involves multi-machine manning and programming, repair and maintenance, and quality inspection. Some craftsmen are now also involved in tool room and design activities. Generally, the trend towards multiple skills to perform varied functions is enhancing the role of craftsmen and technicians in many case studies. Some employers are also redesigning jobs to allow technicians to take on work formerly undertaken by professional staff to improve staff utilisation and counter skill shortages.

In the case of **operatives**, their growing importance in some firms is illustrated by a food manufacturer where skills were upgraded following the introduction of multi-machine manning and first level repair and maintenance.

197

This became possible through the automation of the machine control function. This occupation was regarded as vital because it was entrusted with significant responsibility for the operation of an expensive plant. In an aerospace firm, **clerical** support staff had become vital because the recent corporate reorganisation integrated the previous 13 divisions into four; each being serviced by a common group of support staff who now co-ordinate the functions of large disparate divisions. Numerically though, the role of clerical staff, expecially those with low level skills, is diminishing in importance.

In the service sectors, **support services** is seen as a particularly important occupational group and total numbers are also large, accounting for 25 per cent of the service sector workforce. The case of a company in the retail sector highlights the vital role of this group. In this company, support services constitute the numerically largest group, accounting for just over 60 per cent of the total workforce. A majority of them are involved in sales, shelf-filling and in general functions at stores. The rest work in a clerical or secretarial capacity, mainly at the head office. Those working in the stores are now required to have four kinds of skills: **social skills**, incorporating innate attributes, for an effective interpersonal communication with customers; **product skills** for facilitating customer counselling; **keyboard and diagnostic skills** for an effective interface with point of sale terminals and the back-office mini computer; and **entrepreneurial skills** to ensure the viability of their store as an independent profit centre. The emphasis on these skills reflects two considerations: the throughput at the check-out is highly variable both during and between days of the week; and customers are becoming more sophisticated. Hence in order to achieve a high utilisation rate, sales employees have to be able to perform sales as well as other functions, requiring a repertoire of low level skills. Clerical staff in the head office now perform a cycle of work associated with a geographical area. This involves all clerical duties associated with the stores' operations - including stock monitoring, arranging distribution, production of cash profiles and preparation of financial data. Such duties require: keyboard and diagnostic skills for computer usage; low level knowledge-based skills in subjects such as marketing, book-keeping and stock control; and analytical skills for the preparation of management information.

In this company, the trend is towards job loading in all support service occupations. In the past, lack of training was regarded as one of the reasons for a high staff turnover. It led to mistakes, frustration and low morale. Now there is a strong recognition that business success depends on high quality sales assistants with requisite skills acquired through on-the-job as well as off-the-job training. Whether heightened awareness of training needs will persist into the future is not clear. What is already clear is the change in attitude towards support services employees - both full- and part-time. The latter are no longer looked upon as a flexible resource, to be turned on and off in response to demand fluctuations. Instead, the tendency is to see them as a permanent resource to be nurtured through varied work experience and as much on-the-job training as possible. The attitude is underpinned by the belief that in the evolving competitive environment, products, shop design and layout constitute only one aspect of success. The other, and probably more important, is the social skills and competence of sales staff.

The experience of this retail company was not unique by any means. In banking and leisure services, too, the case studies highlighted a growing recognition that the support as well as personal services occupations such as cashiers, receptionists and waiters were increasingly gaining a 'front-line' status. This was particularly stressed in those organisations engaged in competitive diversification into insurance, travel and accommodation; involving customer confidence because they are mainly services of 'promissory' nature that involve winning that confidence. Innate attributes, social skills and work experience were increasingly regarded as vital for these hitherto less skill-intensive occupations.

Conclusion

This study has highlighted how employers expect the occupational structure in the UK to change over the period to 1990 (Figure 16.3). Numerically, the most notable features are the increase in professional-based occupations; technicians; multi-skilled craftsmen; and support and personal service occupations, involving part-time employees. The numbers of full-time unskilled jobs will decline significantly.

Qualitatively, a number of occupations are perceived as growing in importance. These include managers, engineers, scientists and technologists, and other professions, particularly data processing, accountancy, and marketing staff where employers are increasingly requiring a major improvement in the quality and breadth of skills. In the case of information technology-related staff, accountants, and marketing staff, employers are also expecting to seek increased numbers of suitably trained and experienced staff.

The importance of multi-skilled craftsmen and many operatives is also increasing because of the applications of new technologies, weakening job demarcations and increased work responsibility. Although their numbers are expected to decline, the skill content of many of these jobs will continue to increase.

Two other occupational groups are also expected to require qualitative improvements: support and personal services, particularly in the service sectors. The skill content of their work is expanding, as is the importance of innate attributes. Employee groups such as cashiers in banks, sales assistants in retailing, and waiters in restaurants are increasingly viewed as a 'front line' resource whose quality enhancement is vital in a growing competitive environment. As the role of small firms and smaller units of large organisation will grow in the economy this will require increasing flexibility by all types of employees.

The size of the overall workforce is unlikely to change significantly over the rest of this decade. However, across a large number of occupations, employers see the need for qualitative changes as a result of changing market pressures, new technologies and better working methods. Their central thrust is towards improved work performance, greater knowledge intensity, multiple skills, innate attributes, work experience, and greater flexibility. This applies particularly to management and professional staff who employers, in all types and sizes of organisations, view as a key to business success in a changing environment.

References

Atkinson J & Meager N — Flexibility in Firms: A Study of Changing Working Patterns and Practices; National Economic Development Office; forthcoming.

Bruno M — World Shocks, Macroeconomic Response and the Productivity Puzzle; NBER Working Paper No 342; 1982.

Bruno M & Sachs J — Input Price Shocks and the Slowdown in Economic Growth: Estimates for UK Manufacturing; Review of Economic Studies 49 (311); 1982.

Central Statistical Office — Economic Trends, various issues; Social Trends, 1986 Edition.

Connor H & Pearson R — Information Technology Manpower into the 1990's; Institute of Manpower Studies; 1986.

Ganguly, P — UK Small Business Statistics and International Comparisons; Small Business Research Trust, London; 1985.

Hewer A — Manufacturing Industry in the 70's: An Assessment of Import Penetration and Export Performance; 1982.

HM Treasury — The Government's Expenditure Plans 1986-87 to 1988-89; HMSO, Comnd 9702-1; 1986.

Institute of Employment Research — Review of the Economy and Employment, 1985, Volume 1; 1985.

National Institute of Economic Research — National Institute Economic Review, No 115; February 1986.

Petit P — Slow Growth and the Service Economy, Francis Pinter; 1986.

Rajan A — New Technology and Employment in Insurance, Banking and Building Societies: Past Experience and Future Prospects; Gower; 1985.

University of Liverpool — Quarterly Economic Bulletin, Vol 7, No 1; March 1986.

Appendices

APPENDIX A
THE IMS/OSG SURVEY

IMS

Institute of Manpower Studies

Survey on Employment Prospects
of the UK Economy

As you will see from the enclosed letter from Sir Austin Bide and colleagues, the Institute is undertaking a major research programme for the Occupations Study Group to examine employment trends in the UK in the mid and late 1980's. The critical part of this programme will be to draw on employers' experiences and expectations of employment change in their own establishments and companies. Your co-operation will therefore be an important part of this work.

We would be most grateful if you would complete the attached questionnaire and return it to the Institute in the enclosed pre-paid envelope. If you are able to answer only some of the questions, this would be most helpful. In most cases, the answer involves ticking the appropriate boxes.

All replies will be treated in the strictest confidence. No individual organisation will be identified in our final report which will present the findings in terms of broad industrial and occupational groups. All respondents will be sent a copy of the summary report when it is available. If you have any queries please contact Dr. David Parsons (Survey Director) or Monica Haynes at the Institute. Thank you for your consideration.

Yours sincerely,

Richard Pearson

Richard Pearson
Associate Director

May 1985

IMS, Mantell Building, University of Sussex, Falmer, Brighton BN1 9RF.
Telephone: Brighton (0273) 686751

No. 931547, Registered in England.   Registered Office: 20 Essex Street, London WC2R 3AL

Industrial Coverage

This questionnaire applies to organisations principally engaged in manufacturing, extractive and construction activities.

There is a separate questionnaire for service activities. Please let us know if that is more relevant to your organisation.

1. BACKGROUND INFORMATION

A   What are the main products/services covered by your organisation's business activities?

    ....

    ....

(1-4)

1 (5)

(6-7)

B   Is your organisation a subsidiary of another organisation?   YES ☐
     (Please tick one box)   NO ☐

     If 'Yes', please give the name and country of origin of the parent organisation.

    ....

    ....

(8)

C   How many plants/establishments does your organisation currently operate in
     the UK?   *(Please give the approximate number in the box)*   ☐

(9-12)

2. RECENT TRENDS IN EMPLOYMENT AND BUSINESS

A   How many employees did your organisation have in the UK at the   1983 ☐
     beginning of 1983 and how many does it have now? *(Please enter
     total·number **including** part-time employees in the appropriate boxes)* NOW ☐

(13-18)

(19-24)

B   What happened to the **proportion** of the following categories within your organisation's total
     UK employment between the beginning of 1983 and now?
                                        (Please tick one box for each category)

SINCE BEGINNING-1983 HAS ....

PROPORTION OF:	Increased	Remained Static	Decreased	
(i) Part-time employees				(25)
(ii) Temporary and short-term employees				(26)
(iii) Female employees				(27)
(iv) Young employees (age under 21)				(28)

C   What was the general trend in the following aspects of your organisation's business between
     the beginning of 1983 and now? *(Please tick one box for each aspect)*

SINCE BEGINNING-1983 HAS ....

ASPECTS OF BUSINESS:	Increased	Remained Static	Decreased	
(i) Turnover (net of inflation)				(29)
(ii) Share of exports in turnover				(30)
(iii) Share of sub-contracted business in turnover				(31)
(iv) Product/service range				(32)
(v) Number of customers				(33)
(vi) Productive capacity				(34)

3. RECENT CHANGES IN TECHNOLOGY AND WORKING METHODS

A   What do you consider is the current level of your organisation's adoption of new technologies in each of the following areas? *(Please tick one box for each area)*

NB   *By new technologies we mean product and process innovations, whether based on microelectronics or other applications.*

THE CURRENT LEVEL OF ADOPTION OF NEW TECHNOLOGIES IN:	Is Consider-able	Is Limited	Is Neglig-ible	
(i) Office functions				(35)
(ii) Production processes				(36)
(iii) Components and materials				(37)
(iv) Storage, packaging and distribution				(38)
(v) Others *(Please specify)*				(39)
....				(40)

B   What has happened to the following aspects of your organisation's working methods between the beginning of 1983 and now? *(For each aspect, please tick the appropriate box)*

SINCE BEGINNING-1983 HAS.......

ASPECTS OF WORKING METHODS:	Improved	Remained Unchanged	Worsened	
(i) State of restrictive practices				(41)
(ii) Amount of surplus manning, if any				(42)
(iii) Quality of management				(43)
(iv) Organisational structure				(44)
(v) Quality of equipment and premises				(45)

C   Overall, how do your organisation's current working methods compare with those prevailing at the beginning of 1983? *(Please tick one box)*

MORE EFFICIENT [ ]   UNCHANGED [ ]   LESS EFFICIENT [ ]   (46)

D   As a result of the changes in business, technology and working methods described above, please indicate which **occupations** (if any) have increased or decreased as a **proportion** of your total UK employment? *(Under the appropriate headings below, please list those occupations most affected)*

EXPANDING OCCUPATIONS   CONTRACTING OCCUPATIONS

....
....   (47-55)
....
....   (56-64)
....

E   Which occupations, if any, have presented special recruitment problems over the last year? *(Please list the relevant occupations)*

....
....   (63-73)
....

4. FUTURE TRENDS IN BUSINESS, TECHNOLOGY AND WORKING METHODS

A   What do you anticipate will happen to the following aspects of your organisation's business between now and the end of 1989? *(Please tick one box for each aspect)*

IN THE PERIOD 1985-89 ....

ASPECTS OF BUSINESS:	Is Likely to Increase	Is Likely to Remain Static	Is Likely to Decrease	
(i) Turnover (net of inflation)				(6)
(ii) Share of exports in turnover				(7)
(iii) Share of sub-contracted business in turnover				(8)
(iv) Product/service range				(9)
(v) Number of customers				(10)
(vi) Productive capacity				(11)

B   What do you anticipate will be the extent of your organisation's adoption of new technologies in the following areas between now and the end of 1989? *(Please tick one box for each area)*

IN THE PERIOD 1985-89 WILL BE ....

ADOPTION OF NEW TECHNOLOGIES IN:	Large Extent	Limited Extent	Neglig- ible	
(i) Office functions				(12)
(ii) Production processes				(13)
(iii) Components and materials				(14)
(iv) Storage, packaging and distribution				(15)
(v) Others *(Please specify)*				(16)
....				(17)

C   What do you anticipate will happen to the following aspects of your organisation's working methods between now and the end of 1989? *(For each aspect, please tick the appropriate box)*

IN THE PERIOD 1985-89 WILL ....

ASPECTS OF WORKING METHODS:	Improve	Remain Unchanged	Worsen	
(i) State of restrictive practices				(18)
(ii) Amount of surplus manning, if any				(19)
(iii) Quality of management				(20)
(iv) Organisational structure				(21)
(v) Quality of equipment and premises				(22)

D   Which of the developments identified above are likely to have **most** influence on your organisation's employment level between now and the end of 1989? *(Please list them and, if possible, give details)*

....

....

....

....

5. FUTURE TRENDS IN OCCUPATIONAL EMPLOYMENT

A   In the light of the developments identified in Question 4, what do you anticipate will happen
to your organisation's employment level in the UK in the period up to 1989? *(Only broad
orders of magnitude are needed. If you can give numbers for only one date, please do so)*

	END-1987	END-1989
TOTAL UK EMPLOYMENT NUMBERS ANTICIPATED AT		

_____ (39-44)

_____ (45-50)

B   What will happen to the proportion of the following categories in your total UK employment
in the period up to 1989, in the light of the developments identified in Question 4?
(Please tick one box for each category)

IN THE PERIOD TO END-1989 . . . .

PROPORTION OF:	Is Likely to Increase	Is Likely to Remain Static	Is Likely to Decrease	
(i) Part-time employees				(51)
(ii) Temporary are short-term employees				(52)
(iii) Female employees				(53)
(iv) Young employees (age under 21)				(54)

C   In the light of the developments identified in Question 4, what do you anticipate will happen
to the occupational structure of your organisation's employment in the period up to 1989?
*(The occupational groups listed below are defined on page 8. For each group **relevant** to your
organisation, please give approximate numbers employed now and indicate the likely future
trend by ticking the appropriate box. If you can indicate the trend only for fewer occupations
or for total employment, please do so)*

_____ (1-4)

_____3 (5)

OCCUPATIONAL GROUPS:	APPROXIMATE NUMBERS IN EMPLOYMENT NOW	Is Likely to Increase	Is Likely to Remain Static	Is Likely to Decrease	
(a) Managers and Administrators					(6-11)___(12)
(b) Engineers, Scientists and Technologists					(13-18)___(19)
(c) Other Professions					(20-25)___(26)
(d) Technicians and Draughtsmen					(27-32)___(33)
(e) Craftsmen					(34-39)___(40)
(f) Operatives					(41-46)___(47)
(g) Support Services					(48-53)___(54)
(h) Personal Service Occupations					(55-60)___(61)
(i) Others *(Please specify)*					(62-67)___(68)
. . . .					(69-74)___(75)
					(1-4)_4_(5)
TOTAL					(6-11)___(12)

D   Which occupations, if any, are likely to increase most in the period up to 1989?
(Please list such occupations)

. . . .

. . . .   _____ (13-21)

. . . .

E   Which particular occupations are likely to be most vital to your organisation's future business
performance? *(Please list such occupations)*

. . . .

. . . .   _____ (22-30)

. . . .

212

6. OTHER COMMENTS

Are there other factors currently affecting or likely to affect your organisation's employment level and its occupational structure in the period up to the end of 1989? *(If so, please list them)*

(31

(32

(33

(3⁴

7. FURTHER CONTACTS

Thank you for completing this questionnaire. We may like to discuss with you certain aspects of your answers. If necessary, may we please contact you again?

YES [   ]   NO [   ]

(3ɛ

If 'Yes', please give the name of contact, position and telephone number:

....

....

....

Please return this questionnaire in the reply paid envelope to:

Institute of Manpower Studies, Mantell Building, University of Sussex, Falmer, Brighton BN1 9RF

EXPLANATORY NOTES ON OCCUPATIONAL GROUPS ADOPTED IN THIS SURVEY

The nine occupational groups adopted in the Survey are listed below. Examples of occupations in each group are given alongside.

BROAD OCCUPATIONAL GROUPS	EXAMPLES OF OCCUPATIONS WITHIN GROUPS
(a) Managers and Administrators	Production, sales, personnel and other managers and administrators; proprietors and partners.
(b) Engineers, Scientists and Technologists	Civil, mechanical, electrical and electronic engineers; work study, progress, planning, production and other engineers; metallurgists, chemists, pharmacists, physicists, biologists, etc.; technologists; surveyors and architects.
(c) Other Professions	Instructors, training officers, medical workers, social and welfare related workers; valuers, accountants, solicitors, journalists and other professional workers.
(d) Technicians and Draughtsmen	Technicians, draughtsmen and laboratory assistants. Should include persons carrying out functions of a grade intermediate between scientists/technologists and skilled craftsmen/operatives, whether in research or development, design, production, testing or maintenance.
(e) Craftsmen	
: foremen and supervisors	Engineering foremen and transport inspectors and supervisors.
: engineering	All skilled workers in engineering, electrical and electronic trades (e.g. turners, fitters, welders, tool-makers, motor mechanics, precision instrument makers).
: transferable	Woodworkers, painters and decorators, bricklayers, masons and plasterers.
: non-transferable	All craft workers with industry-specific skills (e.g. miners, potters, furnacemen, jewellers, skilled textile and clothing workers).
(f) Operatives	
: skilled	Riggers, electroplaters, inspectors (metal and electrical), bakers, butchers, printers, other skilled workers.
: others	Surface mine and quarry workers; gas, coke and chemical workers; semi-skilled pottery workers; semi-skilled textile, construction and transport workers; fettlers, machine tool operators, assemblers, press workers, boilermen.
(g) Support Services	
: clerical	Clerks, cashiers, office machine operators, typists, secretaries, telephone and telegraph operators.
: sales	Salespersons (distribution), roundsmen, commercial travellers and salesmen.
(h) Personal Service Occupations	
: security	Security guards.
: personal service	Porters, housekeepers, waiters, bar staff, cooks, canteen assistants, kitchen hands, caretakers and cleaners.
(i) Others	(To be specified by respondents)

Institute of Manpower Studies

Survey on Employment Prospects
of the UK Economy

As you will see from the enclosed letter from Sir Austin Bide and colleagues, the Institute is undertaking a major research programme for the Occupations Study Group to examine employment trends in the UK in the mid and late 1980's. The critical part of this programme will be to draw on employers' experiences and expectations of employment change in their own establishments and companies. Your co-operation will therefore be an important part of this work.

We would be most grateful if you would complete the attached questionnaire and return it to the Institute in the enclosed pre-paid envelope. If you are able to answer only some of the questions, this would be most helpful. In most cases, the answer involves ticking the appropriate boxes.

All replies will be treated in the strictest confidence. No individual organisation will be identified in our final report which will present the findings in terms of broad industrial and occupational groups. All respondents will be sent a copy of the summary report when it is available. If you have any queries please contact Dr. David Parsons (Survey Director) or Monica Haynes at the Institute. Thank you for your consideration.

Yours sincerely,

Richard Pearson

Richard Pearson
Associate Director

May 1985

Industrial Coverage

This questionnaire applies to organisations principally engaged in service activities.

There is a separate questionnaire for manufacturing, extractive and construction activities. Please let us know if that is more relevant to your organisation.

1. BACKGROUND INFORMATION

_____ (1-4)

A   What are the main products/services covered by your organisation's business activities?

.... _____ 1 (5)

.... _____ (6-7)

B   Is your organisation a subsidiary of another organisation?   YES [   ]
    (Please tick one box)   NO [   ] _____ (8)

    If 'Yes', please give the name and country of origin of the parent organisation.

    ....

    ....

C   How many sales outlets/branches/establishments does your organisation
    currently operate in the UK?   *(Please give the approximate number in the box)*   [   ] _____ (9-12)

2. RECENT TRENDS IN EMPLOYMENT AND BUSINESS

A   How many employees did your organisation have in the UK at the   1983 [   ] _____ (13-18)
    beginning of 1983 and how many does it have now? *(Please enter
    total number **including** part-time employees in the appropriate boxes)*   NOW [   ] _____ (19-24)

B   What happened to the **proportion** of the following categories within your organisation's total
    UK employment between the beginning of 1983 and now?
    (Please tick one box for each category)

SINCE BEGINNING-1983 HAS . . . .

PROPORTION OF:	Increased	Remained Static	Decreased	
(i) Part-time employees				(25)
(ii) Temporary and short-term employees				(26)
(iii) Female employees				(27)
(iv) Young employees (age under 21)				(28)

C   What was the general trend in the following aspects of your organisation's business between
    the beginning of 1983 and now? *(Please tick one box for each aspect)*

SINCE BEGINNING-1983 HAS . . . .

ASPECTS OF BUSINESS:	Increased	Remained Static	Decreased	
(i) Turnover (net of inflation)				(29)
(ii) Share of sub-contracted business in turnover				(30)
(iii) Product/service range				(31)
(iv) Number of customers				(32)
(v) Number of sales outlets/branches/establishments				(33)

3. RECENT CHANGES IN TECHNOLOGY AND WORKING METHODS

A   What do you consider is the current level of your organisation's adoption of new technologies in each of the following areas? *(Please tick one box for each area)*

NB   *By new technologies we mean product and process innovations, whether based on microelectronics or other applications.*

THE CURRENT LEVEL OF ADOPTION OF NEW TECHNOLOGIES IN:	Is Consider-able	Is Limited	Is Neglig-ible	
(i) Office functions				(34)
(ii) Production processes				(35)
(iii) Components and materials				(36)
(iv) Storage, packaging and distribution				(37)
(v) Others *(Please specify)*				(38)
......				(39)

B   What has happened to the following aspects of your organisation's working methods between the beginning of 1983 and now? *(For each aspect, please tick the appropriate box)*

SINCE BEGINNING-1983 HAS ....

ASPECTS OF WORKING METHODS:	Improved	Remained Unchanged	Worsened	
(i) State of restrictive practices				(40)
(ii) Amount of surplus manning, if any				(41)
(iii) Quality of management				(42)
(iv) Organisational structure				(43)
(v) Quality of equipment and premises				(44)

C   Overall, how do your organisation's current working methods compare with those prevailing at the beginning of 1983? *(Please tick one box)*

MORE EFFICIENT [ ]   UNCHANGED [ ]   LESS EFFICIENT [ ]   (45)

D   As a result of the changes in business, technology and working methods described above, please indicate which **occupations** (if any) have increased or decreased as a **proportion** of your total UK employment? *(Under the appropriate headings below, please list those occupations most affected)*

EXPANDING OCCUPATIONS   CONTRACTING OCCUPATIONS

....

.... (46-51)

....

.... (52-57)

....

E   Which occupations, if any, have presented special recruitment problems over the last year? *(Please list the relevant occupations)*

....

.... (58-63)

....

4. FUTURE TRENDS IN BUSINESS, TECHNOLOGY AND WORKING METHODS

A   What do you anticipate will happen to the following aspects of your organisation's business between now and the end of 1989? *(Please tick one box for each aspect)*

IN THE PERIOD 1985-89 . . . .

ASPECTS OF BUSINESS:	Is Likely to Increase	Is Likely to Remain Static	Is Likely to Decrease	
(i) Turnover (net of inflation)				(64)
(ii) Share of sub-contracted business in turnover				(65)
(iii) Product/service range				(66)
(iv) Number of customers				(67)
(v) Number of sales outlets/branches/establishments				(68)

B   What do you anticipate will be the extent of your organisation's adoption of new technologies in the following areas between now and the end of 1989? *(Please tick one box for each area)*

IN THE PERIOD 1985-89 WILL BE . . . .

ADOPTION OF NEW TECHNOLOGIES IN:	Large Extent	Limited Extent	Neglig-ible	
(i) Office functions				(69)
(ii) Production processes				(70)
(iii) Components and materials				(71)
(iv) Storage, packaging and distribution				(72)
(v) Others *(Please specify)*				(73)
. . . .				(74)

C   What do you anticipate will happen to the following aspects of your organisation's working methods between now and the end of 1989? *(For each aspect, please tick the appropriate box)*

IN THE PERIOD 1985-89 WILL . . . .

ASPECTS OF WORKING METHODS:	Improve	Remain Unchanged	Worsen	
(i) State of restrictive practices				(75)
(ii) Amount of surplus manning, if any				(76)
(iii) Quality of management				(77)
(iv) Organisational structure				(78)
(v) Quality of equipment and premises				(79)

D   Which of the developments identified above are likely to have **most** influence on your organisation's employment level between now and the end of 1989? *(Please list them and, if possible, give details)*

(1-4)

2 (5)

. . . .

. . . .

(6-20)

. . . .

. . . .

5. FUTURE TRENDS IN OCCUPATIONAL EMPLOYMENT

A   In the light of the developments identified in Question 4, what do you anticipate will happen
to your organisation's employment level in the UK in the period up to 1989? *(Only broad
orders of magnitude are needed. If you can give numbers for only one date, please do so)*

	END-1987	END-1989
TOTAL UK EMPLOYMENT NUMBERS ANTICIPATED AT		

    (21-26)
    (27-32)

B   What will happen to the proportion of the following categories in your total UK employment
in the period up to 1989, in the light of the developments identified in Question 4?
(Please tick one box for each category)

IN THE PERIOD TO END-1989 . . . .

PROPORTION OF:	Is Likely to Increase	Is Likely to Remain Static	Is Likely to Decrease	
(i) Part-time employees				(33)
(ii) Temporary are short-term employees				(34)
(iii) Female employees				(35)
(iv) Young employees (age under 21)				(36)

C   In the light of the developments identified in Question 4, what do you anticipate will happen
to the occupational structure of your organisation's employment in the period up to 1989?
*(The occupational groups listed below are defined on page 8. For each group **relevant** to your
organisation, please give approximate numbers employed now and indicate the likely future
trend by ticking the appropriate box. If you can indicate the trend only for fewer occupations
or for total employment, please do so)*

    (1-4)
    3 (5)

OCCUPATIONAL GROUPS:	APPROXIMATE NUMBERS IN EMPLOYMENT NOW	EMPLOYMENT IN THE PERIOD TO END-1989			
		Is Likely to Increase	Is Likely to Remain Static	Is Likely to Decrease	
(a) Managers and Administrators					(6-11)___(12)
(b) All Professions					(13-18)___(19)
(c) Support Services					(20-25)___(26)
(d) Personal Service Occupations					(27-32)___(33)
(e) Technicians, Craftsmen and Operatives					(34-39)___(40)
(f) Others *(Please specify)*					(41-46)___(47)
. . . .					(48-53)___(54)
TOTAL					(55-60)___(61)

D   Which occupations, if any, are likely to increase most in the period up to 1989?
(Please list such occupations)

. . . .

. . . .   (62-67)

. . . .

E   Which particular occupations are likely to be most vital to your organisation's future business
performance? *(Please list such occupations)*

. . . .

. . . .   (68-73)

. . . .

6. OTHER COMMENTS

Are there other factors currently affecting or likely to affect your organisation's employment level and its occupational structure in the period up to the end of 1989? *(If so, please list them)*

(74)

(75)

(76)

(77)

7. FURTHER CONTACTS

Thank you for completing this questionnaire. We may like to discuss with you certain aspects of your answers. If necessary, may we please contact you again?

YES [   ]   NO [   ]

(78)

If 'Yes', please give the name of contact, position and telephone number:

....

....

....

Please return this questionnaire in the reply paid envelope to:

Institute of Manpower Studies, Mantell Building, University of Sussex,
Falmer, Brighton BN1 9RF

EXPLANATORY NOTES ON OCCUPATIONAL GROUPS ADOPTED IN THIS SURVEY

The six occupational groups adopted in the Survey are listed below. Examples of occupations in each group are given alongside.

BROAD OCCUPATIONAL GROUPS	EXAMPLES OF OCCUPATIONS WITHIN GROUPS
(a) Managers and Administrators	Production, sales, personnel and other managers; proprietors and partners.
(b) All Professions	
: scientific	Electronic engineers, work study, progress, planning and production engineers, technologists; metallurgists, chemists, pharmacists, biologists; surveyors and architects.
: others	Instructors, training officers, medical workers, social and welfare related workers, valuers, financial agents, accountants, solicitors and other professional workers.
(c) Support Services	
: clerical	Clerks, cashiers, office machine operators, typists, secretaries, telephone and telegraph operators.
: sales	Salespersons, roundsmen, commercial travellers and salesmen.
(d) Personal Service Occupations	
: security	Security guards.
: personal service	Porters, housekeepers, waiters, bar staff, cooks, canteen assistants, kitchen hands, caretakers, cleaners, hairdressers and launderers.
(e) Technicians, Craftsmen and Operatives	
: technicians	Technicians and laboratory assistants. Should include persons carrying out functions of a grade intermediate between scientists and technologists on the one hand and skilled craftsmen and operatives on the other, whether in research or development, design, production, testing or maintenance.
: craftsmen	Transport inspectors and supervisors; all skilled workers in engineering, electronic and electrical trades such as fitters, welders, tool-makers, motor mechanics and precision instrument makers.
	Transferable craftsmen such as woodworkers, painters and decorators, bricklayers, masons and plasterers.
	Non-transferable craftsmen such as jewellers, skilled textile and clothing workers.
(f) Others	(To be specified by respondents).

Appendix A.3   Discussion Guide for Case Studies

1 Background

(a)   Who owns the company and how much influence does the respondent
      have in matters of:

    (i)   recruitment
    (ii)   investment, and
    (iii)   training

2/3   Past Trends in Business, Technology, Working Methods and Employment: 1979-85

(a)   **Business Aspects:** What have been the main changes (and why) in:

    (i)   product/service range
    (ii)   number of establishments/production capacity
    (iii)   investment
    (iv)   output, exports
    (v)   customer base
    (vi)   sub-contracted work
    (vii)   competitive environment

(b)   **Technology:** What kind of technologies have been introduced in the
      following areas and why?

    :   office functions
    :   production processes
    :   components and materials
    :   storage, packaging and distribution
    :   others (specify)

(c)   **Work Aspects:** What kind of changes have been made (and why) in:

    (i)   conditions of work
    (ii)   working methods
    (iii)   organisation of work

    :   vertical/horizontal integration
    :   centralisation/decentralisation

(d)   **Employment:** What have been the main changes (and why) in:

    (i)   numbers employed in UK - cyclical, secular trends
    (ii)   their composition by:

    :   age
    :   sex
    :   locality
    :   full and part-time
    :   temporary and contract

(e)   **Occupations/Skills:** What have been the main areas of growth and decline (and why)?

(f)   **Recruitment:** Have you experienced difficulties in recruiting into growth or other occupations (and why)?

(g)   **Training:** What has been the extent of training/retraining of the existing and newly recruited staff? What factors have necessitated training/retraining?

4.   **Future Trends in Business, Technology and Working Methods: 1985-90**

(a)   **Business Aspects:** What are likely to be the main changes (and why) in:

    (i)   product/service range
    (ii)   number of establishments/production capacity
    (iii)   investment
    (iv)   output, exports
    (v)   customer base
    (vi)   sub-contracted work
    (vii)   competitive environment

(b)   **Technology:** What kind of technologies will be introduced, where and why?

(c)   **Work Aspects:** What kind of changes are likely (and why) in:

    (i)   conditions of work
    (ii)   working methods
    (iii)   organisation of work

    :   vertical/horizontal integration
    :   centralisation/decentralisation

5.   Future Trends in Occupational Employment: 1985-90

    (a)   **Employment Forecasts:** In the light of answers to 4 above, what is likely to happen to:

        (i)   the UK-based employment level in end-1987 and end-1989
        (ii)   its full/part-time composition
        (iii)   its sex composition
        (iv)   its temporary, contract composition

    (b)   **Occupational Breakdown:** Consistent with the forecasts above, what occupations are likely to increase and which are likely to decrease; and why?

    (c)   **Key Occupations/Skills:** What are likely to be the key occupations/skills, and why?

    (d)   **Resourcing of Needs:** How do you expect to resource the projected manpower needs?

    (e)   **Implications:** What implications does (d) have for:

        (i)   company's own recruitment and training policies
        (ii)   local labour market and training institutions

    (f)   **Error Margin:** How much error margin should we allow for due to:

        (i)   the potential errors in the forecast method used
        (ii)   the likely variability in the assumptions in 4

    (g)   **Alternative Assumptions:** Which are the key assumptions in 4 from the point of view of employment forecasts and what alternative outcome on them is most plausible?

    (h)   **Variant Forecasts:** Under alternative assumptions, what will be the most likely level of employment?

    (i)   **Sensitivity of Occupational Mix:** Is the mix sensitive to changes in the assumptions in 4? If yes, how and why? If not, why not?

6.   Other Comments

Agricultural and Allied Workers Group (TGWU)
Association of British Offshore Industries

British Association of Professional Hairdressing Employers
British Clothing Industry Association
British Independent Steel Producers Association
British Paper & Board Industry Federation
British Printing Industries Federation
British Textile Employers Association
Building Employers' Confederation
Building Societies Association

Chemical Industries Association Limited

Engineering Employer's Federation

Federation of Civil Engineering Contractors
Food Manufacturers' Association

Institute of Chartered Accountants in England and Wales

The Law Society
Local Government Training Board

National Farmers Union
Newspaper Publishing Association
The Newspaper Society

The Retail Consortium
Road Haulage Association

Society of British Aerospace Companies
Society of Motor Manufacturers and Traders

Timber Growers UK

UK Offshore Operators Association

Appendix A.5   Industrial Sectors and Their Composition

Sectors:	1980 SIC Class
Primary Industries	
(1) Agriculture, Forestry, Fishing	01-03
(2) Energy and Water Supply	11-14; 15-17
Manufacturing	
(3) Process Industries	21-24; 25-26
(4) Engineering and Related Industries	31; 32; 33-34; 37; 35-36
(5) Light Production Industries	41-42; 43-35; 46; 47-49
Construction	
(6) Construction and Allied Industries	50
Services	
(7) Distributive, Financial and Business Services	61-65; 81-85
(8) Transport and Communication	71-78; 79
(9) Leisure and Related Services	66; 97; 67; 94; 98
(10) Public Services	91-93; 95-96

Appendix A.6   Distribution of Survey Respondents by Sectors and Employment-Size

SECTORS:	EMPLOYMENT-SIZE GROUPS								TOTAL
	Below 50	50–99	100–199	200–499	500–999	1,000–5,000	Over 5,000	Unclassified	
	Percentages*								Numbers
Primary and Energy Industries									
1. Agriculture, Forestry, Fishing	-	-	-	-	-	-	-	-	
2. Energy and Water Supply	30	23	13	15	5	5	10	-	40
Manufacturing									
3. Process Industries	11	13	16	19	17	19	4	1	234
4. Heavy Production Industries	19	13	15	22	17	11	3	1	641
5. Light Production Industries	17	15	17	21	14	11	2	2	623
6. Construction	13	13	34	13	10	12	5	-	61
Services									
7. Distributive, Financial and Business Services	29	19	16	14	9	10	3	1	796
8. Transport and Communication	30	18	13	18	6	10	4	2	146
9. Leisure and Related Services	25	25	16	13	6	8	6	1	277
Unclassified	17	17	17	17	8	8	-	17	12
Sub Totals									
: Production (1+2+3+4+5+6)	17	14	17	21	15	12	3	1	1599
: Services (7+8+9+10)	28	21	15	14	8	9	4	1	1231
Total	22	17	16	18	12	11	3	1	2830

* These relate to the row total in the final column

228

Appendix A.7 Distribution of Survey Respondents by Regions

	Production Industries	Services	Total
	Percentages*		
Scotland	8	8	8
North West	10	7	8
North East	5	3	4
Yorks/Humber	11	7	9
East Midlands	9	4	6
West Midlands	13	7	10
Wales	4	2	4
South	9	11	10
East Anglia	5	6	5
South East	6	7	6
South West	7	8	7
London	9	26	16
Northern Ireland	4	3	4
Unclassified	1	1	1
Total	1,599	1,231	2,830

* These relate to the column totals in the final row.

Source : IMS/OSG Survey

APPENDIX B
SELECTED NATIONAL STATISTICS

Appendix B.1 Import Penetration*: 1978-84

(percentages)

Sector:	1978	1979	1980	1981	1982	1983	1984 Provisional
(1) Agriculture, Forestry Fishing	21.0	19.9	18.6	19.1	18.8	17.3	17.7
(2) Energy and Water Supply	24.2	22.3	20.3	17.9	16.5	14.6	16.2
(3) Process Industries	25.7	28.4	33.2	29.1	31.1	32.5	33.5
(4) Heavy Production Industries	23.5	27.3	30.1	32.1	34.9	37.2	38.1
(5) Light Production Industries	18.2	20.0	20.2	19.6	22.2	23.1	25.3
(6) Construction & Allied Industries	0.1	0.1	0.1	0.1	0.1	-	-
(7) Distributive, Financial and Business Services	2.4	2.5	2.5	2.3	2.5	2.3	2.3
(8) Transport and Communication	15.7	16.2	16.5	16.3	16.0	15.9	15.4
(9) Leisure and Related Schemes	4.4	5.4	6.6	7.3	7.0	6.8	6.5
(10) Public Services	-	-	-	-	-	-	-

* Defined as

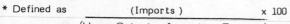

$$\frac{(\text{Imports})}{(\text{Home Output} + \text{Imports} + \text{Exports})} \times 100$$

Source: Central Statistical Office, Commodity Flow Accounts

Appendix B.2 Export/Output Ratios: 1978-84

(percentages)

Sector:	1978	1979	1980	1981	1982	1983	1984 Provisional
(1) Agriculture, Forestry Fishing	5.2	5.0	5.0	6.4	5.9	6.1	7.0
(2) Energy & Water Supply	11.8	15.4	16.2	19.5	21.1	22.7	24.1
(3) Process Industries	22.8	22.7	26.4	26.1	26.1	26.2	26.8
(4) Engineering and Related Industries	26.9	25.7	27.9	29.1	28.6	24.8	26.1
(5) Light Production Industries	11.0	11.2	12.1	11.5	11.5	11.3	11.7
(6) Construction	0.6	0.5	0.4	0.4	0.3	0.3	0.3
(7) Distributive, Financial & Business Services	7.2	7.2	7.3	7.3	7.3	7.2	7.3
(8) Transport & Communications	17.4	16.2	16.7	14.5	13.5	12.5	12.0
(9) Leisure & Other Services	4.5	5.0	6.2	6.7	6.0	6.3	6.4
(10) Public Services	-	-	-	-	-	-	-
Total Great Britain	13.2	13.3	14.0	14.1	14.1	13.7	14.1

Source: CSO

234

Appendix B.3   Retail Trades: Alternative Estimates of Employment

(thousands)

Employees in Retail Trades:	1971	1976	1978	1980	1982	1984
BSO Estimates	2,270	2,118	2,105	2,038	1,950	1,950
DE Estimates	1,951	2,023	2,061	2,134	2,018	2,091

Source: Employment Gazette, Historical Supplement No.1 April 1985;
        Business Monitor, SDA 25

APPENDIX C
FURTHER ANALYSES IMS/OSG SURVEY

Appendix C.1 Energy, Manufacturing and Construction Sectors: Expanding, Contracting and
          Hard-to-Fill Occupations: 1983-85

	Percentage of Mentions					Total
	Energy	Process Industries	Heavy Production Industries	Light Production Industries	Construction	
Expanding Occupations						
Managers and Administrators	12	13	10	13	18	12
Engineers, Scientists and Technologists	20	23	28	17	15	23
Other Professions	5	5	4	5	7	5
Technicians and Draughtsmen	12	11	15	9	6	12
Craftsmen	10	14	15	14	18	14
Operatives	20	12	16	22	6	17
Support Services	22	17	12	16	11	15
Personal Service Occupations	-	-	-	1	4	1
Others	-	6	-	3	16	3
	N = 41	N = 285	N = 760	N = 635	N = 55	N = 1776
Contracting Occupations						
Managers and Administrators	15	6	7	7	2	7
Engineers, Scientists and Technologists	5	3	5	3	12	4
Other Professions	-	2	4	4	2	4
Technicians and Draughtsmen	-	4	6	4	2	5
Craftsmen	5	11	18	12	23	15
Operatives	35	38	32	38	21	35
Support Services	40	30	26	28	19	27
Personal Service Occupations	-	2	3	2	2	2
Others	-	4	-	3	17	2
	N = 20	N = 260	N = 635	N = 489	N = 52	N = 1456
Hard-to-Fill Occupations						
Managers and Administrators	12	18	11	17	23	15
Engineers, Scientists and Technologists	36	33	34	18	13	27
Other Professions	8	10	6	8	17	7
Technicians and Draughtsmen	4	9	13	8	8	11
Craftsmen	12	13	16	17	23	16
Operatives	4	5	11	17	2	12
Support Services	6	13	9	12	15	11
Personal Service Occupations	-	1	-	1	-	-
Others	-	-	-	3	-	1
	N = 25	N = 200	N = 200	N = 656	N = 48	N = 1439

Source: IMS/OSG Survey

Appendix C.2 Oil Industry: Occupational Changes in Period 1985-89*

(percentage)

	Likely To:		
	Increase	Remain Static	Decrease
a. Managers and Administrators	20 (Small)	69 (Small/Medium)	11 (Large)
b. Engineers, Scientists, Technologists	52 (Small)	42 (Small/Medium)	6 (Large)
c. Other Professions	9 (Small)	73 (All)	18 (Large)
d. Technicians and Draftsmen	40 (Small)	56 (All)	4 (Large)
e. Craftsmen	26 (Small)	57 (Small/Medium)	17 (Large)
f. Operatives	46 (Small)	36 (Small/Medium)	18 (Large)
g. Support Services	30 (Small)	40 (Small/Medium)	30 (Large)
h. Personal Service Occupations	12 (Small)	70 (Small/Medium)	18 (Large)
i. Others	31 (Small)	61 (Small/Medium)	8 (Large)

*   Under each percentage is given the type of employers dominating the result. Four employer-types have been designated for this purpose: **Large,** (over 500); **Medium,** (200-499); **Small,** (under 200); **All,** (no dominance by size)

Source: IMS/OSG Survey

Appendix C.3 Process Industries: Occupational Changes in Period 1985-89*

(percentage)

	Likely To:		
	Increase	Remain Static	Decrease
a. Managers and Administrators	18 (Small/Medium)	63 (All)	19 (Large)
b. Engineers, Scientists, Technologists	47 (All)	47 (All)	6 (Large)
c. Other Professions	17 (Small/Medium)	73 (All)	10 (Large)
d. Technicians and Draftsmen	30 (All)	58 (All)	12 (Large)
e. Craftsmen	31 (All)	44 (All)	25 (Large)
f. Operatives	27 (Small/Medium)	23 (Small/Medium)	50 (Large)
g. Support Services	19 (Small/Medium)	43 (All)	38 (Large)
h. Personal Service Occupations	4 (Small)	74 (All)	22 (Large)
i. Others	27 (All)	38 (Medium)	35 (Medium/Large)

* Under each percentage is given the type of employers dominating the result. Four employer-types have been designated for this purpose: Large, (over 500); Medium, (200-499); Small, (under 200); All, (no dominance by size)

Source: IMS/OSG Survey

Appendix C.4 Engineering and Related Industries: Occupational Changes in Period 1985-89*

(percentage)

	Likely To:		
	Increase	Remain Static	Decrease
a. Managers and Administrators	25 (Small/Medium)	60 (All)	15 (Large)
b. Engineers, Scientists, Technologists	33 (Small/Medium)	36 (Small/Medium)	31 (Small)
c. Other Professions	22 (All)	71 (All)	7 (Large)
d. Technicians and Draftsmen	52 (All)	38 (All)	10 (Large)
e. Craftsmen	38 (All)	41 (All)	21 (Large)
f. Operatives	42 (Small/Medium)	27 (All)	31 (Large)
g. Support Services	25 (Small/Medium)	48 (All)	27 (Large)
h. Personal Service Occupations	10 (Small)	72 (All)	18 (Large)
i. Others	30 (Small)	54 (All)	14 (Large)

* Under each percentage is given the type of employers dominating the result. Four employer-types have been designated for this purpose: **Large**, (over 500); **Medium**, (200-499); **Small**, (under 200); **All**, (no dominance by size)

Source: IMS/OSG Survey

Appendix C.5 Light Production Industries: Occupational Changes in Period 1985-89*

(percentage)

	Likely To:		
	Increase	Remain Static	Decrease
a. Managers and Administrators	29 (Small)	59 (Small/Medium)	12 (Large)
b. Engineers, Scientists, Technologists	45 (Small/Medium)	50 (All)	5 (Large)
c. Other Professions	23 (Small)	73 (Small/Medium)	4 (Large)
d. Technicians and Draftsmen	37 (Small)	56 (Small/Medium)	7 (Small)
e. Craftsmen	35 (Small/Medium)	47 (Small/Medium)	18 (Large)
f. Operatives	45 (Small)	23 (Small/Medium)	32 (Large)
g. Support Services	33 (Small)	45 (Small/Medium)	22 (Large)
h. Personal Service Occupations	12 (Small/Medium)	74 (Small/Medium)	14 (Large)
i. Others	29 (Small)	29 (Small)	42 (Medium)

* Under each percentage is given the type of employers dominating the result. Four employer-types have been designated for this purpose: Large, (over 500); Medium, (200-499); Small, (under 200); All, (no dominance by size)

Source: IMS/OSG Survey

Appendix C.6 Construction: Occupational Changes in Period 1985-89*

(percentage)

		Likely To:		
		Increase	Remain Static	Decrease
a.	Managers and Administrators	34 (Small)	51 (All)	15 (Small/Medium)
b.	Engineers, Scientists, Technologists	57 (Small/Medium)	35 (All)	8 (Small)
c.	Other Professions	39 (All)	53 (All)	8 (Small)
d.	Technicians and Draftsmen	45 (Small)	42 (Small/Medium)	13 (Large)
e.	Craftsmen	49 (Small)	33 (Small/Medium)	18 (Large)
f.	Operatives	47 (Small)	36 (Small/Medium)	17 (Large)
g.	Support Services	31 (Small)	58 (Small/Medium)	11 (Large)
h.	Personal Service Occupations	26 (Small/Medium)	74 (All)	-
i.	Others	- -	100 (All)	- -

* Under each percentage is given the type of employers dominating the result. Four employec.-types have been designated for this purpose: **Large**, (over 500); **Medium**, (200-499); **Small**, (under 200); **All**, ,no dominance by size)

Source: IMS/OSG Survey

Appendix C.7 Service Sectors: Expanding, Contracting and Hard-to-Fill Occupations 1983-85

	Percentage of Mentions					
	Distributive Financial and Business Services	Transport and Communication	Leisure Services	Other Services	Public Services	All Services
Expanding Occupations						
Managers and Administrators	17	16	22	11	10	17
Other Professions	31	16	17	27	50	28
Technicians and Draughtsmen	16	25	11	25	20	18
Support Services	33	37	21	30	10	31
Personal Service Occupations	3	5	28	6	10	6
Others	1	-	1	1	-	2
	N = 649	N = 109	N = 88	N = 89	N = 10	N = 955
Contracting Occupations						
Managers and Administrators	10	10	28	6	13	11
Other Professions	10	7	11	11	-	10
Technicians and Draughtsmen	28	34	8	41	50	29
Support Services	48	47	25	36	38	45
Personal Service Occupations	2	3	28	5	-	4
Others	1	-	-	2	-	1
	N = 449	N = 73	N = 36	N = 64	N = 8	N = 637
Hard-to-Fill Occupations						
Managers and Administrators	17	20	23	13	16	18
Other Professions	34	26	10	35	42	30
Technicians and Draughtsmen	15	15	7	25	11	15
Support Services	32	40	17	22	26	30
Personal Service Occupations	1	-	44	5	5	7
Others	1	-	-	1	-	1
	N = 546	N = 76	N = 105	N = 86	N = 19	N = 839

Source: IMS/OSG Survey

245

Appendix C.8   Distributive, Financial and Business Services:
Occupational Changes in Period 1985-89*

(percentage)

		Likely To:		
		Increase	Remain Static	Decrease
a.	Managers and Administrators	40 (Small/Medium)	53 (All)	7 (Large)
b.	All Professions	52 (Large)	43 (All)	5 (Small)
c.	Support Services	47 (All)	37 (All)	16 (Small)
d.	Personal Servivce Occupations	21 (All)	69 (All)	10 (Small)
e.	Technicians, Craftsmen & Operatives	45 (All)	42 (All)	13 (Small)
f.	Others	52 (Small)	32 (Small/Medium)	16 (Small)

*   Under each percentage is given the type of employers dominating the result. Four employer-types have been designated for this purpose: **Large,** (over 500); **Medium,** (200-499); **Small,** (under 200); **All,** (no dominance by size)

Source: IMS/OSG Survey

Appendix C.9   Transport and Communication: Occupationational Changes in Period 1985-89*

(percentage)

		Likely To:[1]		
		Increase	Remain Static	Decrease
a.	Managers and Administrators	32 (Small)	59 (Small/Medium)	9 (Large)
b.	All Professions	36 (Small)	59 (Small/Medium)	5 (Large)
c.	Support Services	43 (Small)	42 (Medium)	15 (Large)
d.	Personal Service Occupations	33 (Small)	63 (Small/Medium)	4 (Large)
e.	Technicians, Craftsmen & Operatives	53 (All)	32 (All)	15 (Large)
f.	Others	43 (Small)	46 (Small/Medium)	10 (Large)

*   Under each percentage is given the type of employers dominating the result. Four employer-types have been designated for this purpose: Large, (over 500); Medium, (200-499); Small, (under 200); All, (no dominance by size)

Source: IMS/OSG Survey

Appendix C.10 Leisure and Other Services: Occupational Changes in Period 1985-89*

(percentage)

	Likely To:		
	Increase	Remain Static	Decrease
a. Managers and Administrators	36 (Small/Medium)	51 (Small/Medium)	13 (Large)
b. All Professions	39 (Small)	49 (All)	12 (Small)
c. Support Services	33 (Small)	43 (Small/Medium)	24 (Small)
d. Personal Service Occupations	12 (Small)	72 (All)	16 (Large)
e. Technicians, Craftsmen & Operatives	50 (Small)	35 (Small/Medium)	15 (Large)
f. Others	44 (Small)	39 (All)	17 (Large)

* Under each percentage is given the type of employers dominating the result. Four employer-types have been designated for this purpose: Large, (over 500); Medium, (200-499); Small, (under 200); All, (no dominance by size)

Source: IMS/OSG Survey

POSTSCRIPT

At the outset Sir Austin and the OSG recognised that they were setting a challenging objective to explore employment and occupational trends, and their underlying causes, over a five year forecast period. The need for a study was prompted by concern that the regular post war cyclical pattern of job losses followed by compensatory gains may no longer be valid. The feasibility study carried out by the IMS highlighted the complexities involved and the difficulties employers have in looking or planning over a five year period. An implicit objective of the OSG in commissioning the main study was, therefore, to see if such a broad employer-based study could yield useful results for those in industry, education, Government and society.

The main study, reported here, sought to reconcile a broad and diverse data base, derived from employers, into a consistent and coherent framework. Despite the range of uncertainties involved, we believe that the study has been able to present a useful benchmark and to highlight the underlying trends and changes in employment and occupations across the economy, and to explain why employers expect these changes to come about. If some of the current views about causes are not emphasised, it is because employers did not do so.

The findings suggest that the economy is in a period of major occupational change, which is likely to be lengthy. There is clearly a wide range of factors that will affect the outcome over the period to 1990. Time alone will show the precise pattern and timing of change and it may be appropriate to up-date this data base at some time in the future. At present, however, it is for the reader to assess the value of this report in aiding his or her own understanding of employment and occupation trends, and the implications for education, training and society.

Frederick Meredith, Director General, Occupations Study Group

Richard Pearson, Associate Director, Institute of Manpower Studies